PROFITABLE CAREERS IN NONPROFIT

William Lewis
Carol Milano

John Wiley & Sons, Inc.
New York • Chichester • Brisbane • Toronto • Singapore

Publisher: Stephen Kippur
Editor: Katherine S. Bolster
Managing Editor: Ruth Greif
Editing, Design, and Production: Publication Services

Copyright ©1987 by John Wiley & Sons, Inc.

All rights reserved. Published simultaneously in Canada.

Reproduction or translation of any part of this work beyond that permitted by Section 107 or 108 of the 1976 United States Copyright Act without the permission of the copyright owner is unlawful. Requests for permission or further information should be addressed to the Permissions Department, John Wiley & Sons, Inc.

This publication is designed to provide accurate and authoritative information in regard to the subject matter covered. It is sold with the understanding that the publisher is not engaged in rendering legal, accounting, or other professional service. If legal advice or other expert assistance is required, the services of a competent professional person should be sought. FROM A DECLARATION OF PRINCIPLES JOINTLY ADOPTED BY A COMMITTEE OF THE AMERICAN BAR ASSOCIATION AND A COMMITTEE OF PUBLISHERS.

Library of Congress Cataloging-in-Publication Data

Lewis, William, 1946–
   Profitable careers in nonprofit.

   Bibliography: p. 194
   1. Vocational guidance—United States.
2. Corporations, Nonprofit—United States. I. Milano, Carol. II. Title.
HF5382.5.U5L44   1987   331.7'02   87-6102
ISBN 0-471-83699-0

Printed in the United States of America

10 9 8 7 6 5 4 3

Contents

	Introduction	iv
1	How Nonprofits Differ from Other Corporations	1
2	The World of Nonprofit	5
3	Finding Your Place Among Nonprofits	15
4	The Executive Director	27
5	The Development Office	47
6	The Program Department: Providing the Service	61
7	Membership and Publications	113
8	Public Relations	136
9	The Administrative Areas	148
10	Government: The Nation's Largest Employer	159
11	Targeting, Exploring, and Getting a Job	172
	Appendixes	
A	Associations	190
B	References	194
	Index	200

Introduction

The typical urban career-change workshop of the 1980s attracts two distinct types of participants. In one group are artists, health-care workers, educators, and members of other creative or "helping" professions, seeking higher incomes—whether or not they still love the work they have been trained to do. An equal-sized but very different faction is the corporate white-collar crowd, yearning after 12 or 16 years of big business to "do something that matters." Comparing experiences and realities in a group format can help group members clarify their goals and puncture their grass-is-always-greener fantasies.

After six or eight weeks, a workshop participant may conclude that he or she is in the wrong position or working for the wrong employer, but need not change fields or directions. Workers in nonprofit organizations frequently discover they do not belong in the corporate sector and would actually be happiest where they are (perhaps because, to their surprise, they would actually be paid less in a new career that they currently earn!). A great awakening befalls businesspeople, who listen to the intangible rewards afforded by many nonprofit careers and realize that any potential loss of income would be more than offset by the opportunity to perform meaningful work more in keeping with their personal values.

Not enough information is available to help job seekers or prospective career changers evaluate the nonprofit realm adequately. Because nonprofit organizations are generally somewhat "low profile" in terms of recruitment activities, advertising, and image-building, job hunters tend to be less aware of the activities and opportunities available. We would like to offer corporate career changers, new college graduates, mothers reentering the job market, and all interested individuals an honest look at the realities of a career in nonprofit, where 23 percent of America's work force is employed. As with any career decision, it is important to appraise both the positive and negative features; our book attempts to be unbiased and thorough in portraying the views of dozens of nonprofit employees.

The nonprofit universe is surprisingly wide and varied, and even in a full-length book, we have had to be selective about which areas to include. For example, while both the clergy and the military are large and important not-for-profit employers, we did not feel that a reference book—no matter how well intended and sincere—could or should serve as the determinant for such personal and complex decisions. Similarly, while government at federal, state, and local levels is the largest employer in America and is by definition not-for-profit, we have elected not to focus heavily on government positions (although one short chapter is devoted to them.) We discovered it is impossible to discuss careers in health or education, two classic nonprofit fields, without explaining the role of government programs that hire high percentages of professionals in these areas.

The first three chapters of our book describe the nonprofit universe, in terms of its population, services, characteristics, unique features, and the range of entities within it. In Chapter 3, you can assess how well your interests and values match up with opportunities in the nonprofit world. Chapters 4 through 9 provide portraits of the executive director position, the development office, the program departments, membership activities, publications, public relations, and all the administrative services, including finance, accounting, personnel, office management, and data processing. Chapter 10 gives a brief overview of government jobs. The last chapter will help you identify a career goal and pursue it successfully.

For the most part, we have tried to examine jobs possessing the qualities a motivated, reasonably educated adult might seriously consider. We have omitted the blue-collar positions found in not-for-profits because the work itself varies little from similar positions in commercial enterprises. In fact, because the nature of a given job tends to remain constant across different types of organizations, we have arranged the section that looks at specific employment areas by position, rather than by the type of service the organization provides. A fund raiser for a small private school, for example, has essentially the same set of responsibilities as the vice president for development of a large hospital; only the dollar amounts vary, not the nature of the work itself.

We have a special interest in the world this book covers, since both of our mates have chosen not-for-profit careers. In addition, coauthor Carol Milano, who started her professional life at a national student association, coordinates a training program for fund raisers today. We hope this book gives you a clear, fair picture of an evolving, rewarding sector of American society.

1
How Nonprofits Differ from Other Corporations

NOT FOR PROFIT DEFINED

People are often confused by the term *not for profit*. Does it mean that you work for no pay? Or that services are given away for free? Are nonprofits the same as charities? Can they pay their bills? What do they do with the money contributors give them?

Let's answer these important questions. The term *not for profit* means that the organization does not intend to earn profits from its activities. A not-for-profit corporation has a State Certificate of Incorporation allowing it to operate legally. It must have a board of directors and a clearly defined aim or mission. A not-for-profit organization is permitted by law to hire people to carry out its goals; these people receive salaries, benefits, and reimbursements for legitimate expenses, just as employees in the for-profit sector do. All of the same withholdings, such as disability and unemployment insurance deductions, appear on their paychecks. (Social Security is optional.) At the end of the year, however, any profits earned must be poured back into programs, equipment, and space for the organization, rather than being divided among the employees. This means that, unlike the profit-making companies traded on American stock exchanges, not-for-profits cannot pay dividends to their shareholders (in fact, there are no shares or shareholders) or bonuses to their workers. The board of directors, or trustees, serve without pay.

Because budgets are leaner and service orientation is stronger in a not-for-profit than in most other corporations, volunteers are generally welcomed. It does take staff time to train and supervise volunteers, so they may not be the most efficient means to accomplish a goal. However, they provide free labor for a cause they care about, and many nonprofits, especially the smaller ones, could not manage without them. These organizations have learned to use humanpower in lieu of capital.

"For-profit corporations make decisions based on net present value," said Lisa Leinbach, the development officer at the National Council on Alcoholism. "Cost factors are not the determinant in a not-for-profit. We may know a loss will occur, but still need to do a project because of the organization's goals. Decisions in not-for-profit are made on softer criteria, such as how many lives will we save?"

Not all nonprofits are charities. Some, of course, like the Salvation Army or the Red Cross, provide their services at no cost to the recipients. But any parent paying the tuition bills at Bennington, Harvard, or Tulane is unlikely to feel those nonprofit institutions are "giving it away." Apart from colleges, many institutions, including museums, churches, and YMCAs, receive a large portion of their budgets from membership fees, dues, or offerings from congregation members. Other organizations, such as hospitals or the ASPCA, do not have memberships to offer and must solicit contributions from the public in order to operate. A registered not-for-profit is the only kind of operation permitted to have a fund raiser soliciting donations on behalf of the organization, and those donations are tax deductible for the donor.

Contributions must, by law, be spent by the organization to which the donation was made.

Unlike for-profit businesses, which must pay taxes on their income just as individuals do, not-for-profit businesses are exempted from the obligation to pay taxes, in recognition of the fact that the organization's activities are in the public interest.

Nonprofits are sometimes referred to as 501(c)3 groups, an Internal Revenue Service (IRS) Code classification that also allows them to accept grants from the government or foundations, as well as receiving tax-deductible contributions from other donors. However, nonprofits are also restricted by the IRS from attempting to influence legislation and from any involvement in political campaigns. What is more, when a nonprofit business is dissolved, its assets *must* be transferred to another tax-exempt organization, rather than being distributed among the directors or officers.

The board of directors of a nonprofit must have three or more members, who meet at least once a year. They set the organization's policies, elect officers, and see that the mission of the nonprofit corporation is being carried out. The executive director is hired by and reports to the board. Usually, the board has significant fund-raising responsibilities and must make sure that an annual report is produced.

American businesses, of course, are active lobbyists. While 501(c)3 organizations are restricted politically, there is one category of not-for-profit, the 501(c)4, that is permitted to lobby on behalf of civic, educational, charitable, recreational, and cultural causes. Because contributions to this type of group are not tax deductible, lobbying organizations are supported by members' dues.

According to Tim Jensen, staff attorney at Volunteer Lawyers for the Arts, "If benefits flow *out* to the public, the organization gets tax-deductible status. Unions and some professional groups, where benefits flow inward, are not 501(c)3. The 501(c)4 category means tax exempt, but not tax deductible."

Who is watching to make sure nonprofits are maintaining their legal responsibilities? The IRS requires annual reports and other documentation that the organization is continuing its services to the public. Other tax returns and reports are required at the state level. When government agencies or foundations have made a grant, they generally ask for updates or status reports during the course of the grant work. The board of directors is responsible for reviewing financial statements each year. The National Charities Information Bureau (NCIB) was founded in 1918 to "maintain sound standards in philanthropy, and to provide advisory services to contributors." They evaluate more than 300 national organizations and make their findings available at no charge to prospective donors. National agencies are encouraged to meet the NCIB's standards.

2

The World of Nonprofit

INTRODUCTION

Look around your immediate world for 24 hours and you will soon discover that nonprofit organizations are everywhere, although you may not yet think of them that way. The Boy Scouts in your community, the church on the corner, the town's historical society, your local library, the senior citizen's center, and the museum, school, or hospital you pass each day are all not-for-profit organizations.

What do all of these, and many more, institutions have in common? And what is it that they actually do? According to Bill Olsen, former headmaster of a large, independent coeducational boarding school, "Nonprofits share a concern for the quality of life, and they perform a public service. The typical nonprofit is private, independent, and not directly controlled by a government agency."

Nonprofits take care of basic human needs, providing food, clothing, and shelter to the homeless, handicapped, or elderly. They tend toward medical and health problems, seeking cures and new forms of treatment for a full range of diseases. They offer education and social-welfare services. They try to inform the public and organize communities around legal, political, and ethical issues. Nonprofits provide art and culture and attempt to preserve our environment and our various heritages. Churches and temples bring us spiritual guidance, while other nonprofits guide community development, growth, and renewal.

While we have come across nonprofit organizations that do virtually everything imaginable, the one constant is that they all offer assistance in some way to some population. These are the helping, giving, caring service fields, comprising over 270,000 service organizations. They are also in businesses, however, having raised $79. 8 billion from the public in 1985.

An individual not-for-profit can operate with a very specific goal or a broad array of aims. A large church, for example, may provide not just religious activities for its members, but also an assortment of community services ranging from hot meals for the poor, to self-help meetings for alcoholics, to resettlement services for refugees. The local library provides books, magazines, and perhaps films or records to its constituency. It may also conduct literacy programs, English-as-a-Second-Language courses, workshops on job interviews, or discussion groups in the evening for community residents, besides presenting productions by an amateur theater group and mounting exhibits of art or photography by local residents. The Girl Scouts of the United States of America are committed to "fully developing the potential of each member," and strive to "help today's girls become productive, self-confident, socially responsible women," through career education, sports programs, leadership development, and science orientation.

A myriad of smaller, less famous organizations exist, many of which have very specialized, though equally strong, commitments. The Treehouse Wildlife Center near St. Louis, for example, was founded in 1980 to care for orphaned or injured wild animals and help them return to the wilderness.

Its staff cares for more than 300 animals and birds each year. The Starlight Foundation, founded in 1983, tries to grant the wishes of critically, chronically, or terminally ill children. It has provided children with everything from a family trip to Hawaii to a guest appearance on television. The Computer Museum in Boston was set up in 1982 to display the 40-year evolution of the now pervasive computer. The U. S. Lighthouse Society, based in San Francisco, is trying to unify America's scattered lighthouse rescue groups. The society expects to be an information clearinghouse and exchange, as well as a national voice on the topic. New Ventures, a four-year-old agency, provides consulting services to nonprofit businesses that are trying to initiate a revenue-generating operation, such as a bookstore. The Foundation for Long-Term Care, an advocate and information service, reports a growing trend toward intergenerational day care on both national and local levels. They keep track of programs serving both the elderly and children from infancy through kindergarten age which provide the two populations with separate activities as well as shared pastimes, such as singing or watercolor painting. Opening in 1986, the New Mexico Museum of Natural History will preserve and teach the Southwest's natural history. It is the first new state natural history museum since Idaho launched one in the 1930s. The Rescuarium at the North Wind Underseas Institute in New York is saving seals brought to them by the New England Aquarium. The institute, housed in a sea captain's Victorian mansion, is visited by 12,000 schoolchildren each year. The Hartford Architecture Conservancy, whose name indicates its focus, also supplies information to area homeowners on where to buy materials for restoring older homes. Membership has doubled, from 600 to 1,200, in the past five years. The Museum of Broadcasting in New York City, founded in 1975, preserves and presents achievements from television's past to the public. In short, no matter what your particular interest or concern, a not-for-profit somewhere in America addresses it.

Nonprofits come in every shape, size, and site. They operate in the tiniest towns, the largest cities, and everywhere in between. Their headquarters can be a small room lent by another organization, or a sprawling campus, complex, or building. Some nonprofits have chapters in hundreds of locations, while the majority operate in one base. The Princess Grace Foundation, which supports performing artists, has a full-time staff of three; the Smithsonian Institution, with an annual budget of $76 million, employs 3,100.

HISTORY OF NONPROFITS

The ancient Greeks contributed the word *philanthropy*, which means love and concern for one's fellow man, but it has become a characteristically American pastime. Initially, America followed the example of England in the eighteenth and nineteenth centuries, when private philanthropy responded actively to the social needs brought about by the Industrial Revolution. In the late 1800s, a spate of welfare laws were enacted in this country through the efforts of such crusaders as Chicago's Jane Addams. The federal government began to acknowledge an increased social responsibility and encouraged corporations and foundations through tax incentives to take a more active interest in the public well-being. Actually, federal support for nonprofit ventures began in 1803, when Congress funded the Lewis and Clark expedition. In 1842, the federal government made its first specific grant, one of $30,000, to Samuel Morse to test his telegraph system for public use.

It was not until 1967, when David Rockefeller's prodding led to the establishment of the Business Committee for the Arts, that the corporate world officially assumed some of the responsibility for cultural funding. By 1981, corporate contributions to cultural organizations reached nearly $400 million annually. Minneapolis has been the pacesetter for corporate contributions, with the Dayton-Hudson Company encouraging other large Minneapolis businesses to give the full 5 percent of profits the law allows for philanthropy. Indeed, the city has a "5 Percent Club."

In both England and America, however, individuals have always dominated philanthropy. Today, nonprofit organizations receive about 80 percent of their funds from individual donors. Many of our great philanthropic foundations were founded at the turn of the century, before the introduction of income tax, when American entrepreneurs, like Andrew Carnegie and John D. Rockefeller, were amassing huge personal fortunes. Charitable giving was widely practiced by many of these individuals. Colleges and universities, of course, sprang up in America's earliest years. However, it was 1890 before a university, Yale, set up an alumni fund to raise money for the school.

Benjamin Franklin is our nominee for the "Godfather" of philanthropy in America. In addition to his scientific and diplomatic achievements, Franklin was deeply committed to social welfare. He signed his first published articles, while still a teenager, "Mrs. Silence Dogood," reflecting the underlying puritanical ethics of his culture. One of his early social-improvement projects was the founding of a society (the Junto Organization) to debate moral, political, and philosophical questions, and exchange information about business that might be valuable to members. He helped establish the University of Pennsylvania and the Pennsylvania Hospital, and set up a fire company in Philadelphia. He organized the world's first subscription library, which purchased its books from members' contributions and circulated them for free. Franklin created both the first city postal system and the dead-letter office. Showing the depth of his commitment to charitable giving, when Franklin was named Postmaster General of the United States in 1775, he donated his salary to help wounded Revolutionary War soldiers.

NONPROFITS TODAY

While Benjamin Franklin made significant contributions in the areas of health, education, culture, civic affairs, and social welfare, today the public does not support all these categories of not-for-profits equally. The American Association of Fund-Raising Counsel surveys philanthropic contributions each year. According to their 1985 report, the nation's giving for the previous year was distributed as follows:

Religious organizations	47.9 percent
Health and hospitals	14.0 percent
Education	13.5 percent
Social welfare	10.8 percent
Arts and humanities	6.2 percent
Civic and public groups	2.8 percent
Miscellaneous other organizations	4.7 percent

The reason religious groups get such a big portion of the philanthropic pie is that they ask for contributions every week of the year. Churches and temples spend as much money to meet human and social needs as corporations and foundations do. Religious organizations have three levels of involvement in human services: a congregation can provide direct assistance to the needy; it can offer cash or in-kind contributions to other service providers; and religiously affiliated funding federations, such as Catholic Charities or the Federation of Jewish Philanthropies, can contribute to service programs. Among the services provided directly by religious institutions are basic necessities, like food and shelter; support activities, including counseling or recreation; and caretaking, in nursery or school programs.

Education is likely to be an area that is familiar to you, since approximately one out of four Americans is directly involved in this activity. In the mid 1980s, elementary and secondary education includes 57.2 million students, 3.3 million teachers, and 300,000 superintendents, principals, and supervisors in both public and private spheres. Elementary school enrollments had been declining since the 1970s and well into the 1980s, leading to a better pupil-teacher ratio. While enrollments have recently begun to climb again, the improved ratio is now an accepted part of the educational system. The projected need for teachers shows increasing job opportunities.

Two main categories exist among nonprofit hospitals and health-care organizations: government-funded community or general hospitals (which employ over 3 million people) and voluntary not-for-profits, with over 2.2 million workers. In recent years, publicly funded hospitals have remained constant in number but grown larger in patient population. In the civic category, more money has been going to rural development or environmental groups.

Because they serve the public need, nonprofits reflect and respond to changes in American society. For example, the March of Dimes, a highly successful and well-known organization, found its goals accomplished when accessible, almost universally available polio vaccine essentially eradicated the disease in the 1950s. Rather than go out of business, the March of Dimes retained its methods and general purpose, but shifted its focus to become instead the March of Dimes Birth Defects Foundation.

The National Association for the Advancement of Colored People (NAACP) has made impressive gains since its beginning in 1909. Now it has a budget of nearly $11 million, but membership fluctuates widely, from a high of 550,000 in the 1970s to a number below 450,000 in the mid 1980s. As a cost-cutting measure, the NAACP, which has always rented office space in New York City, is buying and renovating a building in Baltimore in hopes of saving $500,000. Executive Director Benjamin Hooks, looking forward to the NAACP's first "home site," hopes its new conference center will become the "Camp David of black America." Aside from a drop in membership, the NAACP has to counter the view that it is no longer the premier civil-rights leader. Its focus, according to Hooks, has shifted to "trying to make sure that the laws now in place are enforced." The organization's greatest challenge these days is a more sophisticated set of problems: after the legislative changes the NAACP helped bring about, the organization now has to attain economic gains for its constituency in a more conservative era.

With 1,700 branch offices, the NAACP remains one of the best-known and most stable forces in the black community, but it, too, must adapt to changing times and criticisms.

America's need for lighthouses has dwindled, because large boats depend on sophisticated equipment and small vessels can be guided by comparatively inexpensive automated beacons. Perhaps 1,000 lighthouses still stand along the nation's coasts, half of them operated by the Coast Guard and another 50 tended by the National Park Service. All the lighthouses will be automated before 1990, eliminating maintenance costs, but residents of many seaside communities do not want to see their shorefront landmarks abandoned and crumbling. A grassroots movement has begun in many towns, with local organizations striving to "adopt" their lighthouses by raising the money to lease them from the Coast Guard. Under this sort of arrangement, the community group promises to restore and maintain the lighthouse for its own use. In some cases, the structures themselves generate part of the upkeep costs if they are turned into nautical museums, bed-and-breakfast inns, or picnic facilities.

Abandoned lighthouses garner little national publicity, but you probably *have* been reading about the emerging problems of America's increasing homeless population. A 1986 conference in Philadelphia attracted 200 representatives from 15 states and most of the biggest cities. The representatives generally agreed that the national estimate of 500,000 to 3 million homeless is, by any count, growing. Mayor Wilson Goode, who organized the conference, saw it as the birth of a nationwide coalition to mobilize efforts that will permanently reduce the number of homeless. Goode hopes the coalition will convince Congress to provide sufficient aid. Today's homeless are more likely to be merely poor, rather than derelicts, and an increasing percentage are families and young people. The underlying social features contributing to homelessness are rising housing costs and shifts in the economy. Increasing numbers of people are finding themselves unable to afford housing because of health problems or their lack of the job skills needed in a service-oriented, high-technology labor market. Advocates for the homeless agree that the long-term solution will have to involve affordable permanent housing; for the present, however, new shelters are opening continously, under the auspices of assorted private and government nonprofit agencies. Three years ago, the Ethical Culture Society in a gentrifying urban neighborhood began running a shelter for single men. Each weekday night, from mid November through April, ten homeless individuals are given soup and sandwiches, a night of safe sleeping, and breakfast the next morning. A rotating crew of volunteers staffs the shelter, and the community contributes food. One mayor claims his city is now sheltering more people than they did during the Great Depression. With the plight of the homeless likely to persist for a while, more religious and social service agencies will be directing new or greater efforts towards assisting them.

Some categories you may not think of as not-for-profit are part of this universe, too. Foundations, for example, which provide grants to nonprofits, currently employ about 6,000 people. America's 23,800 foundations distribute over $4.5 billion each year, but only 1,500 have any paid staff. Private foundations, in fact, generally have fewer than five employees. Some 30 to 40 highly endowed, well-staffed foundations offer a more structured work environment and better compensation than their smaller counterparts. The Ford Foundation, for example, has its own building, employs 340 people, and makes grants in the range of $85 million a year. Because they give money to not-for-profit organizations, foundations occupy a unique position within this sector; interestingly, many foundations also have a development staff to raise additional funds for the organization to distribute. The March of Dimes Birth Defects Foundation, the Princess Grace Foundation, and the United Negro College Fund are in this group.

Labor unions are another unusual unit within the nonprofit world. Severe membership declines in the "smokestack" industries have been offset by gains in service areas, education, health, government, and the high-tech fields.

Union activities serve their own members rather than the general public, so they do not have all the privileges to which nonprofits are legally entitled, but they certainly exist to assist their constituencies rather than to earn a profit for their founders.

Trade associations, similarly, provide a service to their members and are set up as not-for-profit organizations. The American Institute of Certified Public Accountants, the American Bar Association, the Modern Language Association, and the American Medical Association are some of the trade organizations you have probably heard of. Aside from producing publications and membership directories, they offer continuing education classes for members (and non-members, at a higher fee), provide credentials, and act as spokespersons for the industry and sources of information for the public. Associations operate on members' dues, gifts from donors, revenue from publications and conferences, and income from merchandise. Many have a paid staff, often with more than one branch office. Washington, D.C., is the unofficial capital of professional associations, which like to be near government decision-making bodies to keep members' interests represented in the national legislative forum.

As the examples in this chapter make clear, nonprofits add a dimension of caring, culture, and concern to our lives that would otherwise be sorely missed. Now that you have an overview of the world of nonprofit, you need to assess whether or not a career in nonprofit is right for you and determine what opportunities exist.

3
Finding Your Place Among Nonprofits

TRAITS OF NONPROFIT EMPLOYEES

Any career-related decision calls for honest self-assessment. Before you can identify the nonprofit niche where you would be happiest, you will have to determine what you want from your work, in general. There is no question that the biggest distinction between profit-sector and not-for-profit career paths is in the nature of the employee's commitment. Commercial real estate brokers and investment bankers, for example, are often motivated by extravagant earning potential, whereas teachers look first at the opportunity to inspire students.

Bill Olsen, who recruits high-level professionals in the nonprofit fields for the executive recruiting firm Russell Reynolds, Inc. , asks his clients to look in the mirror and say, "What gets me excited? What's my real motivation?" Olsen notes that nonprofit employees tend to be driven more by cause than by tangible rewards. "The executives I place want to do something good for society. They believe in what

Planned Parenthood does, or they want to help find a cause for cancer. Teachers want to help kids. They share a general interest in improving the quality of life, and they're spiritual, not materialistic."

Another important trait for anyone considering nonprofit work is a concern for people and their well-being. Loners will not be happy in this business, unless they are proposal writers. "You need empathy, sensitivity, curiosity, extroversion, and a well-developed sense of what's right and wrong," states Linda Broessel, who recruits not-for-profit executives at a consulting firm called The Oram Group.

Sarita Gupta, fund raiser for the American Friends Service Committee, concurs. "The best thing about nonprofit is that when you get up in the morning, you are in some small way contributing to society. I haven't sold my soul for money. Working for this organization keeps me connected to ideals I had in my youth, while I'm a professional and earning a living at it."

Adhering to your ideals is a central concern for satisfied nonprofit professionals. In a career-change workshop, long before she shifted from an executive job in the travel industry to psychiatric social work, Gail Martino wondered, "How many years can you dedicate all your creative energy to trying to sell shampoo?" Martino, who plans to become a therapist, earns one-third of her former salary now, but feels certain she made the right choice, in terms of her own values.

Michael Jones, now a National Public Radio (NPR) station development director, has worked for a variety of nonprofits in several states. From his diverse experience, Jones has assembled the following composite of the individual who succeeds in nonprofit:

> They share creativity and commitment, and tend to be well-educated and well-read. They like people–although not necessarily dealing with them. Financial managers, for example, don't have to deal well with people. I see a lot of "hippies that grew up"–those who wanted to change the system and saw nonprofit as a way to do so, with a healthy dose of realism. It

helps to be what I call a "warrior," from the American Indian concept of putting the interests of the tribe above your own, and defending the culture.

THE NONPROFIT WORKPLACE
Rewards of Nonprofit

What are some of the "intangible" rewards of nonprofit work? The joys of nonprofit for Karen Szurek, of the Museum of Broadcasting, are "fun, great coworkers, and enthusiasm." Flo Porter, at the Wellness Community in Santa Monica, also cites coworkers as a great reward of her work. "It's nonthreatening and noncompetitive here. We wear casual clothes, in a cozy atmosphere." Previously, she spent five years at a local bank, helping customers get their houses out of foreclosure. "In the bank," she compares, "everyone was out for the promotion. Here, I keep my stress level down. There's much less pressure in nonprofit." She also likes the sense of being part of a team and the ongoing cooperation.

Tim Jensen, of Volunteer Lawyers for the Arts, notes that while he and many of his coworkers worry about the relatively low prestige accorded to nonprofits, the trade-off is "to feel good about what you do. Lots of people feel neutral about their work; here we have people who believe in what they're doing, despite the lower pay. A lot of highly paid people do things at work they don't respect morally."

Employees in most not-for-profit organizations know they would probably earn more in the business world, and many people we interviewed were candid about their financial concerns. Before making your own decision, consider the choice of Alice Chebba and see if she is expressing your values, as well. Involved with theater since high school, Chebba is now fiscal manager at the Alaska Repertory Theater. She enjoys nonprofit work for the following reasons:

> You know people aren't in it to make money. Everyone is dedicated to the field, and likes the work they do. Sometimes

I'm disturbed by the low pay, especially on a frustrating day. I'll find myself thinking, why am I going through this much aggravation when I could be working for IBM and making four times as much money? I never wanted to be rich. I only wanted to be happy. If I could be rich and happy, that would be great! Usually the good points outweigh the bad.

The situation is hardly unbearable, though, for Chebba points out, "I'm making enough now for a nice apartment, nice clothes, saving a little, and taking a nice vacation each year."

People who shifted into nonprofit from corporate careers often make the most eloquent comments about the benefits of their new field. Maryann Alfano was an office manager at an apparel sales firm before joining the International Center for the Disabled. In comparing the two positions, she remarks:

> The corporation was very structured, very black and white. Nonprofit has many different ways to do things, more leeway, and greater challenge. You can be innovative and use your own skills. You feel like you're doing something, even though the pay is so much less. I took a $10,000 pay cut at first. You have to love it, or it would be crazy to make all these sacrifices. The atmosphere is more relaxed in nonprofit, so the work environment is more pleasant. Everyone knocks themselves out for the same reason.

Formerly a vice president for customer service at a large bank, Joe Bartol now heads a banking and finance department at a private university. He finds less pressure, more autonomy, and, perhaps surprisingly, more prestige in the academic setting:

> When...you're a vice president at one of the larger banks, there are so many the significance diminishes. There may be 2,000 vice presidents in a huge bank, and far fewer directors in a university. Once you pass the point of economic obsolescence, a profit-making company will look for someone with more current skills to do the job. In a very large business

organization, you have much more specialization. At the university, I'm a generalist; all the functions report to me.

Over and over, nonprofit professionals applaud the chance to be generalists. Steve Bajardi, another former banker, declares, "Nonprofit is more diverse. The variety of things to do and experiences you have is much broader. Large corporations tend to specialize. You do *one* thing. Nonprofit requires you to be a generalist, rather than a specialist. The diversity is exciting."

Why all this emphasis on varied responsibilities? Because of tighter budgets, Tim Jensen finds:

> A nonprofit requires versatility. Everyone cooperates. You answer the phone in a small organization—you can't afford people to do only one thing. With a staff smaller than it could be, you have to be willing to do things that aren't in your job description. You can't be stuffy. If people need help, you have to be willing to do it. Many people in nonprofit have decided they want their work to be defensible in terms of the contribution to society. It helps to be people-oriented. You're a service organization, so you deal with people. Be very flexible.

As all of these statements make clear, the two keys to satisfaction in the nonprofit world are (1) a deep commitment to the organization for which you work, and (2) absolute certainty that your primary goal is not money.

Nonprofit and Corporate Differences

Subtle differences between corporate and nonprofit organizations abound. Bryan Knapp left the corporate personnel field after 15 years and moved to a university administration post where "it took a long time to catch the rhythm. The university, for example, is required to take the lowest bid for printing. In business, you pay to get things done. The school has no slush fund. You can't get more money for important things."

Another significant distinction is the difference in tone between for-profit and nonprofit organizations. Former corporate budget director Gail Martino remembers her previous companies as "very impersonal, unfeeling. Emotions were never expressed. For a woman in finance to talk about feelings would be taken as meaning she wasn't 'one of the boys.'" Now Martino works with psychiatric patients at a city hospital, serving as an advocate. "It's challenging intellectually and emotionally. In nonprofit, I sometimes feel I have more control. I can bring out the potential for change, so my input is more immediate and direct. I make a contribution. In business, the reward is not so immediate; your contribution is limited."

Yet another banker, Fred Hart (his name has been changed at his request), coordinates employee chemical dependency programs at a prestigious urban hospital. For five years before this, while earning his Ph.D. in counseling psychology, he was the manager of employee assistance programs for a multinational financial services corporation. Hart compares the two jobs as follows:

> The bank was like living in a foreign country, for nearly five years...I was very isolated at the bank, where we had thousands of employees in 90 countries. I saw bank employees in Washington, California, and Minnesota to help employee assistance programs in those sites. Fifteen percent of my phone calls were outside the city I worked in. Hardly anyone at headquarters was in a field allied to mine. It was very lonely. I dealt with people who didn't understand my language or values system.
>
> Relative to the bank, [the hospital] is a small organization with easier lines of access to the top. What health-care executives consider heavy politics is light stuff to me.... Working for a bank, your product is money. As a human services professional, you've chosen to be trained in an area other than accounting or finance, since your values don't run that way. You're always the poor cousin. For the bank to become a treatment facility would ruin it financially. Their goal was to do the bare minimum to keep employees productive. Management measures the work produced by an employee,

so there's little support for employees per se. At the hospital, the product is health care. The president of this institution has taken the Hippocratic oath. The bank's CEO took the business oath: do anything for profit. Anyone I talk to at the hospital understands good treatment is the essential issue. The aggressive business ethic conflicts with human service. Top corporate people often flaunt influence or money, and may try to pressure you.

"It's a lot more human in nonprofit," Tim Jensen agrees. "Most organizations realize that because they pay a little less, they need to give more in terms of vacation schedules, etc. The interpersonal atmosphere is better, more cordial, in a small hierarchy."

Those great vacations are cited nearly as often as the diversity of a nonprofit job. Because it is hard for a nonprofit to give lavish salaries or raises, they reward employees with time off, which doesn't cost the organization actual dollars. The Foundation Center, a specialized library, gives all employees five weeks off in addition to the usual holidays. "We get great vacations," exclaims NPR's Michael Jones. "It's three paid weeks, and our everyday schedules are very flexible. While it's not 9 to 5 here, we do work more than 40 hours a week." Frank Sherman, at Trinity College, gets five weeks off each year, and notes that the faculty have even longer vacations. Joe Bartol gets five or six vacation weeks at his university job, and cites free tuition as another valuable benefit. Bartol's college, like many academic or medical institutions, gives him a nearby apartment and parking spot at much less than market price. He would lose this choice urban bargain if he left the university. Gail Martino has more time off at the hospital (four weeks), but lost all her free-travel benefits by leaving her last industry. However, she notes that "the travel industry is very high pressured, volatile, and unsteady. During budget season, I worked 13-hour days for five months." She now works a little over 40 hours a week.

Do you want longer-than-average vacations and a flexible, varied workday, possibly lasting more than eight hours? Can you adapt to shifting needs and work well as a team member? Again, because it is so important to care deeply about the organization, nonprofit professionals are unlikely to march out at 5 P.M. They take a strong personal interest in their organization's goals, so the tendency is to stay until a task is completed.

Working Conditions in Nonprofit

What about working conditions in nonprofit agencies? In all honesty, they vary widely. Linda Broessel recruits executives for well-established nonprofits, and declares, "The working conditions are usually comparable to corporate environments." Al Milano, at the Cleveland Play House, calls his theater company's complex "unbelievably attractive." Michael Jones finds the "physical surroundings unattractive" at his NPR station but remembers that a former nonprofit employer, the USO, has nice offices. Fred Hart says simply, "The hospital is less plush." The Foundation Center's Candace Kuhta calls her working conditions "excellent." We visited many nonprofits in our research, and most were adequate, pleasant work environments, if not lavish. The nature of some organizations dictates that they will be, to say the least, unusual work environments: zoos, museums, parks, animal shelters, or preschool programs. Colleges are often on campus settings, and libraries are usually freestanding buildings near the centers of their communities. We saw some nonprofits that were both distinctive and inviting. The University of Judaism, in the Hollywood hills, is a group of very attractive modern buildings sprinkled across a naturally green, beautiful site. Sarita Gupta's office at American Friends Service Committee is in the Quaker complex, next to the Friends Seminary. She is in a beautiful red brick building with white pillars, facing a leafy urban park. The Wellness Community, in downtown Santa Monica, is in a cheerful, very nonsterile, homey former house. It is intentionally inviting to patients. Fred Hart moved to a lower-income, noncorporate neighborhood when he left the financial services giant. "I like the street action of the community," he notes now. "I don't miss the fast pace of downtown or midtown. Here I can walk and look around. This is a real residential community, where people live and work." Often, nonprofits are not in the central business district, since that is not the best location for a school, hospital, or social service agency. Rents are higher in these areas, too. At most nonprofits, wardrobes are more casual, and commuting may not involve the usual rush-hour crush.

Drawbacks in Nonprofits

What are some of the other drawbacks of working for a nonprofit, aside from the relatively modest salaries? A frequent lament is outdated or inadequate equipment and lack of space. Often, volunteers could help out with a variety of tasks, but there is no place to put them to work.

Astute emigrés from the corporate world have observed a few other difficulties that afflict nonprofits. After more than 25 years in international marketing for Union Carbide, Frank Sherman chose a second career with his alma mater, Trinity College. He finds decision making is very different in his new job. Whereas decisions tend to be made at the lowest possible level in the profit sector, in nonprofit, decisions are made closer to the top. "Individuals like the president of a college end up making decisions that should be made three levels down. Nonprofits make a lot of decisions by committee—too many. This can take forever, and doesn't always lead to the right decision. Even hiring is done by a committee, which is very inefficient. Nonprofits tend to overemphasize things like affirmative action, and bend over backwards to comply." Any infractions of rules would be highly visible in a small organization, Sherman remarks, partly because they are under close scrutiny since they are supported by public dollars.

Management styles often differ, too. Frank Sherman observes that "businessmen tend to have a tighter style, more structured and well-organized." Joe Bartol, formerly a banking manager, notes his university "doesn't look at itself as a total business environment. Instead (deans say) 'show us the income and then we'll give you the revenues.' " Bartol does feel that he has a great deal of autonomy at the university to design a course or new program. He contrasts this with the situation in the profit sector, where often "the person above you wants credit for the successes, and steals the thunder away."

Steve Bajardi, at the Princess Grace Foundation, cites "a lack of organizational discipline" in nonprofit organizations. "There are more changes, so management is difficult. Corporations do react to strikes, the market, outside occurrences, but at least they have a plan. I find much less long-range planning in nonprofits." He predicts that "increased competitiveness will force nonprofits to be smarter, shrewder, and better managed, or else they won't survive."

Frank Sherman comments that a "nonprofit doesn't have staff help like the profit sector. You must be able to, or learn to, do everything yourself. You don't have the level of advertising help, for example, so you'll have to do the creative work yourself."

Lisa Leinbach, development officer at the National Council on Alcoholism, claims, "People who made it in the business world do come to nonprofits, but their business experience may not work here. Waste goes on in for-profit corporations, as it does in nonprofits. You're not paying for it personally, out of your own pocket, at a corporation. Less margin for waste is built into the smaller budget of a nonprofit, so it shows up more. People aren't given guidelines for expenses."

SUMMARY

We have examined the pros and cons of working for a nonprofit organization. Now, to help you decide if you belong in the not-for-profit sector, we have created two simple self-exploration exercises. The first, a fantasy, will help you begin to see your values and interests, so it is important to answer honestly and open-mindedly:

You have just won $25 million in the state lottery, so you will never have to work again. How will you spend your time? What will you do all day or all week? How will you spend your money? Would you contribute to any philanthropic causes? Which ones?

The second exercise is a little more serious, and asks you to rank order some of your work-related requirements. A self-scoring explanation follows.

Values Inventory

Instructions: Below you will find a list of ten values. In the column, rate each of these on a scale of 1 to 8 according to their importance to you and your career. (8 represents most important; 1 represents least importance.)

                                                              Score   Adjustments

High Income
Prestige
Independence
Helping Others
Security
Variety
Leadership
Interest in Field
Enough Leisure Times
Entrance with a
  Minimum of Preparation

Now, total the number of points you gave each career value.
                                                         Total: _____

Adjustments: In order to help you clarify the relationship of your values to one another, adjust the scores allocated to each until the total equals 40.

Based on this inventory, what are the most important things to you in your job and in your career? What did you learn about your values as you reconsidered them and reassigned point values? Were there any surprises? Have your values changed recently? Why?

We'd like to conclude this chapter with a checklist of the key questions to ask yourself before you decide a career in nonprofit is right for you.

Checklist   *Yes*   *No*

1. Is it important for you to work for a cause?
2. Do you want to do something good for society?
3. Are you more humanitarian than materialistic?
4. Do you have a well-developed sense of right and wrong?
5. Do you have strong ideals?
6. Do you like people?
7. Are you flexible? creative?
8. Would you prefer working for an organization to which you feel committed?
9. Do you want to be part of a team effort?
10. Do intangible rewards truly mean more to you than money?
11. Would you rather be a generalist than a specialist?
12. Are you comfortable working in casual clothing?
13. Does your self-image fit a "noncorporate" work environment?

If you have honestly answered "yes"—especially decisively—to most of these questions, you will probably fit well in the nonprofit world, which the rest of this book will explore in greater detail.

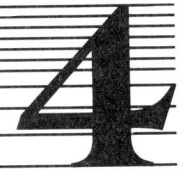

4
The Executive Director

INTRODUCTION

While the job goes by many names—dean, managing director, hospital administrator—every nonprofit has its chief executive officer (CEO), who reports to the board and is in charge of the daily operations of the organization. What does such a job entail?

In the smallest or newest not-for-profits, the executive director may be the only professional full-time staff member, perhaps assisted by a secretary. If the top official has a flair for fund raising or public relations or both, the organization's visibility, resources, and audience evolve steadily. Soon the responsibilities can be divided among one or two other paid professional staff. A skilled, effective, far-sighted, and versatile executive director is the single greatest asset a nonprofit can have. As in any business, when the organization grows, it is important for its CEO to relinquish some of his or her responsibilities by delegating to other capable colleagues.

The right executive director can also move an established

nonprofit to new plateaus. Harvey Lichtenstein, head of America's oldest performing arts center, has just celebrated his twentieth anniversary on the job. When he took over, the Academy of Music was solidly mediocre, with small audiences, underutilized space, and an unfavorable location. This talented administrator has truly put his institution on his city's—and America's—cultural map. By pioneering innovative programs aimed at a broader public, Lichtenstein and his now sizable staff attract fashionable crowds (and funding sources) to their out-of-the-way site on the "wrong side" of the river.

Only a mile away from the Academy of Music, a very small, very old county Historical Society languished in near obscurity for decades, until an aggressive new executive director took over in the early 1980s. He changed the name of the society to narrow its focus and began expanding the staff and the public relations efforts. Society exhibits are now reviewed and listed in the arts sections of all the local publications. New, well-publicized programs are presented to the general public, not just to members. A steady series of walking tours and lectures is offered to attract the affluent professionals now moving into the county. The society is also in the process of expanding its building to create more exhibit space. Membership has increased as the society develops a higher profile. And Executive Director David Kahn is always cited as the catalyst.

Because they are at the top of the hierarchy, the executive directors can get blame as readily as credit when things do not go well. The executive director speaks for the organization. If a problem arises, if the community or constituency is upset, or if the nonprofit falters in providing its service, the executive director is interviewed, quoted, criticized, or accused. This is a highly visible role. With their tax-exempt status and, frequently, substantial base of public support, not-for-profits are closely watched; all buck-passing leads, ultimately, to the executive director's door. Public speaking and diplomacy are very helpful abilities for this position. Regardless of the organization's size or budget, the executive director has the overall day-to-day managerial responsibilities for its operation.

CHARACTERISTICS OF EXECUTIVE DIRECTORS

It is hard to offer a precise portrait of the executive director position. Lew Smith, chief executive officer of America's oldest settlement house, explains:

> Job descriptions are vague because of expectations by clients, staff, and board that the executive director will make things happen. That means many things: setting an image, new programs, connecting with community residents and community groups, working with the board, supervising staff, raising money—making the critical difference.

Smith divides his time between phone calls, letter writing, and meetings. Describing his own style as proactive, he finds that "the job is reactive some of the time. The government funding agency requests a certain report, so we have to react. The greatest difficulty is getting everything done that needs to be done—setting priorities. The most exciting, the hardest, part is doing lots of things at the same time. You must function on a lot of levels, on many projects, all at once."

In his first year on the job, Smith totally revamped the agency's youth programs, providing educational, social, recreational, and counseling activities for kids to replace an amorphous, ineffective program. He added new components, serving junior high school students for the first time in a public school setting. Smith worked closely with a proposal writer, helping to develop ideas. He is highly team oriented and reports heavy staff participation in program development.

Jessica Andrews, who runs the Indianapolis Repertory Theater, defines the job of managing director as "dealing with people, solving problems, leadership, and motivation. I'm not sure that gets taught in school. The problems are the same, whether the organization is large or small. You have to see all the interconnections."

As the executive director of a large suburban temple in Pennsylvania, Marcus Laster is in charge of "fiscal, physical, and management operations, but not religious activities." He hires and supervises the clerical, administrative, and maintenance staff, and puts out a newsletter. "I'm not responsible for the religious service, but I have to make sure the lights are on," he notes. Laster spends over half his time interacting with people, the other half on budgeting and desk work. He often spends a whole day on the telephone, working on such projects as a daylong citywide program on intermarriage. Besides overseeing all of the committees, he handles the publicity and public relations and coordinates the program.

Although his title is director of development, Steve Bajardi is the highest-ranking employee of the Princess Grace Foundation, so in effect he functions as its executive director. Says Bajardi, "I run the office, pay the bills, and coordinate all the foundation's activities. It's tough to make time for development, my main responsibility." Aside from "normal management tasks," he is in charge of writing, public speaking, direct mail, special events, and corporate solicitations.

He is not quite the executive director, but Bryan Knapp is the associate dean of the continuing education school of a large private university. Knapp, previously vice president of human resources in the U.S. Group of American Express, says of his current post, "I am general manager of a small company that offers a quality service in a very competitive marketplace." Describing his responsibilities in corporate terminology, Knapp lists "product development (the curriculum); marketing strategy (looking at jobs, skills, and economic trends); pricing; distribution (classes, conferences, self-study, and video offerings). We should be market-driven here, not product. I'm imbued with a certain capitalistic fervor to return a surplus to the university, offering a decent educational product at the same time."

For 20 years, Bill Olsen was headmaster of a traditional New England prep school, where his domain included 500 students, 65 to 70 teachers, and a support staff of 120. He began his career as a teacher and now recruits executives for nonprofits at Russell Reynolds, an international search firm. His candidates, he states,

> focus more on the program of the organization than on management. They come up through the daily activities of the organization and learn the business side later. . . . .I can point to lots of corporate executives who couldn't make it in nonprofit, where you must persuade people by different methods. The primary asset in nonprofit is leading by example. You have to be persuasive, diplomatic, sensitive and responsive. The executive director may be surrounded by intelligent, independent, strong-willed professionals—try ordering a group of doctors around!

As the descriptions given make clear, the executive director of a nonprofit organization must wear many hats. He or she must also be highly dedicated and prepared to put in long hours. "Most people won't take a high-level nonprofit job if they don't care about the cause," reports Linda Broessel, who recruits executives on three coasts: East, West, and Gulf. According to Broessel, after commitment to the cause, executive directors need "empathy, sensitivity, a well-developed sense of what's right and wrong, curiosity, and extroversion. You have to be sociable. Lots of shy people can counter it," she adds. "Nonprofits pay in satisfaction." Broessel feels the M.B.A. degree can help at the executive director level. "Top executives serve on other boards, as volunteers. We consider whether the executive makes charitable contributions each year. Is he or she willing to mingle with the community?"

Herb Paris, administrator of Brunswick Regional Hospital in Maine, is president of the local United Way and cochairman of both fund raising for the local historical society and the capital campaign for the arts center. He serves on other advisory committees, both local and national, and was formerly on the board of trustees of Brandeis University. "I'm very visible in the community," he remarks. He's even more visible, and very accessible, within the hospital. Normally, his hours are 7:30 or 8 A.M. until 5:30 or 6 P.M. "I may pop in to finish something over the weekend, and I frequently drop in on the evening or weekend staff. People are comfortable approaching me. In a smaller hospital, you have more hands-on involvement and more direct influence over programs."

An arts organization, Jessica Andrews finds, "does not really serve a community, in the way that the Red Cross does, but we are in a neighborhood and hope the community will follow and come to us." She is involved as much as possible in Indianapolis activities and tries to be visible by going to the chamber of commerce and to receptions.

Marcus Laster works a minimum of 50 hours a week, counting evening meetings and weekend activities, including those of the local Federation of Jewish Philanthropies and other community groups. Al Milano, managing director of the Cleveland Play House, states "my staff will sit in on rehearsals of every play—if they don't want to do that, we don't want them."

EVALUATING THE EXECUTIVE DIRECTOR POSITION

Rewards

While this degree of dedication may seem daunting, these same individuals also stress the rewards of their jobs. Milano, who has worked for eight different nonprofits since he finished college in 1965, says "it's never occurred to me to go corporate. I would never do anything other than what I'm doing." Bill Olsen comments that "do-gooder is a pejorative term, but it's the core of the issue. Satisfaction in nonprofit jobs doesn't derive from the money. Leonard Bernstein, while well-paid, thrives on the conducting, not the earnings. These executives are not driven by dollars." Fortunately, they are not starving either. "Nonprofit executives enjoy the things that money can buy, and change jobs for better salaries," Olsen continues. "They seek rewards, not incentives, and believe that the organization will take care of them. Your material needs will be covered while you pursue the mission."

Marcus Laster's reward is the "feeling of satisfaction, facilitating people's opportunity to express their belonging to the Jewish community. Contributing to the survival of Judaism is a key motivator." The fun of the job, he states, is "you never know what will happen next. There's a lot of spontaneity. Every day is totally different, and most of the day is *not* spent at a desk."

Hospital administrator Herb Paris likes "the diversity and the interplay with all levels of the community. The job is generally fun. I'm comfortable in what I do, and with my skills." His biggest reward is productivity. "The quality of life in this community is different from other areas. We get a lot of support from the community, which takes pride in the hospital. They're happy with what they get. We have a mutual dependence." Paris appreciates the "give and take between my responsibilities at the hospital and in the community."

Jessica Andrews thrives on "making a difference. When I guide a group through solving a problem and see the organization move a step closer to the goal, I'm pleased. When an audience member tells me how much he like the play, it's rewarding. The networking all over the country is gratifying, and I like being part of a national theater movement."

Al Milano thrives on challenge, too. He initially hesitated to take the director spot at the Cleveland Play House, because of his reluctance to move north from Dallas and the dullness of the artistic fare. Now in his second year on the job, he comments that "the Play House now has an improving acting troupe. I could never do these plays in the Southwest, nor these playwrights or directors. We're using people from New York and Chicago, since we're one hour by air from each." Formerly reluctant donors are now seeing the potential and beginning to contribute.

Bryan Knapp likes the fact that he is participating in his city's economy in his role as associate dean. He had felt removed from the consumers at American Express (AmEx) and welcomes what he calls "customer contact" during registration periods at the university. His central concern, curriculum development, has easily measured results. "You see immediately whether something works here; two weeks into registration, you can tell. It was harder to gauge the effects of a performance appraisal system at AmEx," he points out. Knapp's role is action-oriented, responding to news of expanding industries.

Problems

Of course, being a nonprofit's CEO is not without difficulties. Marcus Laster is sometimes frustrated by the need to make decisions by committee. "I can't set policy. This is a membership organization, above all, and in our multi-level committee system, the membership is the highest authority. They elect the board of directors and officers, who appoint committees to do research to recommend policy to the board." Bryan Knapp describes the university's orientation as "no sense of urgency, but a constant sense of crisis." He too is often frustrated by the "lack of timely response to requests for information. [The program directors] are academics when it suits them, businesspeople when that suits. Because the staff believes they'd get more money outside, they're casual about other things, like hours. They arrive at 10, leave at 6." This schedule contrasts sharply with Knapp's own; he is always the first person in, arriving at 7:15 or 7:30 A.M. and leaving around 6 P.M. He discovered, to his surprise, that staff members do not always meet deadlines or inform him when they won't—behavior that is unheard of in a corporation. "It's not so warm and integrated in academia," Knapp finds. "With competition limited for promotions and money not lavish, information becomes the source of power, so it's hard to get sharing or collaboration."

Dealing with the board of directors is arguably the most critical, and often the most difficult, part of an executive's role. Explaining the relationship, Bill Olsen says

A nonprofit can operate at a "surplus"—which is not called profits and must be used for the mission of the organization. The board ultimately decides on allocations and makes the big policy decisions, such as letting a school become coed. The executive constructs the actual budget, approved by the board. For example, the board can [allocate] $2 million for salaries, and specific employee rates are then set by the headmaster.

Jessica Andrews has encountered some resistance from the board of directors to allocate more money for staff. "Their perception is that people in the arts do it for a lark, or because it's fun. I believe in giving people what they need to live on, including insurance. . . .If we expect to keep skilled employees, we need to pay them. Fewer people will sweep floors for $50 a week to be an apprentice and watch a director work." Andrews relies on her board members for introductions to prominent members of the community; later on, these residents may be invited to contribute to the Repertory company.

Describing himself as a "good political, corporate-type player in this field," Al Milano left an earlier management post with a major symphony orchestra because of conflicts with the board. "Relationships count for everything in [arts management]; it's not like punching a time clock or looking at the bottom line. If the 'vibes' aren't good, you leave." Earlier in his career, at a management job with a large library, Milano states that "money was on my mind, but dollars had nothing to do with the decisions. In lieu of a raise, I tried to avoid reporting to an inept supervisor."

Management Styles

Management styles in executive director positions can be as varied as the organizations and individuals in question. Jessica Andrews maintains, "People can't feel threatened at including others in the decision process. If you need to decree what will happen, you're lost out here. We put a lot of creative minds together. No one gets paid enough in this business to not feel they have a direct effect on the organization. People must know they make a difference."

Andrews looks for interpersonal skills and a team orientation when she hires. "My staff can see the larger picture and tell me how they'd break up pieces and implement. Lots of people have the techniques, but it's harder to see how to sell something to the community. Practically, how would they do the job?"

Herb Paris does not seek a yes-person, but "someone secure enough not to avoid challenging me. Flexibility is essential: I need someone who can say, 'Okay, I argued my point and so did the other person.' My staff are secure in their skills and independent enough to carry out their responsibilities professionally." He bases hiring decisions on the individual's responsiblity level, degree of responsiveness, and commitment to the welfare of the hospital.

One of Al Milano's main responsibilities is to increase earned income from activities other than Cleveland Play House performances, such as concerts or performances by other theater companies. He divides his staff by function—marketing, public relations, fund raising, and so on—and looks for "people with experience in the specialty, who may have lots of practical online know-how at dealing with people, but not necessarily any theatrical experience. They need not have an arts degree, but appreciation is crucial." Milano maintains that

> the arts are developing new techniques, out of necessity. Telemarketing began in the arts, selling theater subscriptions. I discuss telemarketing and direct mail with businesspeople. Because we don't have money to work with, or people trained at the highest levels, we must get big results out of small investments. Therefore, we have to be better than our counterparts in the corporate sector. . . .The staff needs aggressiveness and dedication to succeed, without resources. . . .Corporations may pay more, but they don't have better people. A lot of nonprofit staff don't realize how skilled they are.

His 15 years in the corporate personnel field (at Union Carbide, First National Bank of St. Paul, Salomon Brothers, and American Express) have given Bryan Knapp a different perspective. While he finds the university setting "appealing and open," he admits missing the "inquisitiveness, intellect, and diverse interests of the American Express staff, a worldly group." In some ways, he found his corporate coworkers quicker to act, and brighter. "Our marketing director is less skilled than a corporate counterpart," he assesses. "Politicking exists here, but it's not sophisticated." He finds his present job relatively unpressured but notes that "some of my directors work harder than I do, preparing course-by-course budgets. The staff need to produce revenues and must meet their budgets. I feel pressure only when I need to go outside my department for collaboration." His last employer dominated his life; Knapp now wants no involvement (yet) with university committees. He really aims "to be home by 6:30 P.M. without a briefcase."

Size of the Organization

Like other businesses, nonprofits vary in size from a staff of one plus a secretary/assistant, to an entire building filled with hundreds of employees conducting activities all over the country. In evaluating an executive director position, one must thus consider the size of the organization. Marcus Laster, having directed both large and small temples, reports that the responsibilities "vary with the perceived priorities of the lay leadership. In a small congregation, the main need may be more money, calling for fiscal management. In a large congregation, the key may be overall coordination of the entire institution, integrating fiscal, human, and physical resources at the same time."

Laster is with a large temple now, in an affluent Philadelphia suburb. When he worked for a smaller community, he found that he missed the collegiality of fellow professionals. "For peer exchange, I relied on long-distance phone calls. In Washington, D.C., or the Philadelphia area, I can meet once a month with a professional association." Laster belongs to the National Association of Temple Administrators (reform), the National Association of Synagogue Administrators (conservative), and the National Association of Church Business Administrators.

"You see the same problems, whether an organization is large or small," Jessica Andrews believes. She left her first job, at the well-established Hartford Stage Company, for a smaller, less sophisticated company in Rochester, seeking the challenge of a less secure setting where her skills could be tested. She found a terrible cash flow and an inexperienced board. "It was a difficult couple of years to build the organization up," she remembers. "I had to answer the phone, lick envelopes, type my own letters. In four years, I accomplished a great deal. I saw the need for a new building and other growth steps, and believed the organization needed to make some big changes." It was time to move on when she "felt someone else could do it better."

Lew Smith, big-city high school principal before he became executive director of the settlement house, notes some parallels between the two positions:

> Most educational literature talks about the critical role of leadership in a school. The same holds true here. An executive director sets a tone. Similarities include playing the key leadership role, establishing priorities, figuring out what needs to be done, putting people in motion to get things done. You have to find the right people for each task, outline an approach, motivate them to do it, provide a sense of support, and reward them for doing it.

In other respects, however, his role as executive director differs in some significant ways from his last post.

> I worry about money here, but didn't have to in a school. As a principal, you don't get quite enough money, and go to the board of education and fight for more. But you get about 95 percent of what you need. I have more accountability here,

bigger budgetary responsibilities, and more creative latitude. The settlement house has a mission to comprehensively serve community residents in ways that help them lead more independent, meaningful lives. It's very broad-based. We might aim, for example, to get kids off the streets. So we design a program, get a grant or funds, and hire the right people. Never in a thousand years could you do that in a school system!

In both roles, though, he has found that the most important decisions he makes involve people.

Salary, Location, and Benefits

What are salaries like in such positions? Generally, the larger the organization, the better the pay. Nonprofit salaries are increasing, as they are in other industries, according to Bill Olsen. "Earnings reflect what an organization can afford, or get away with. Grass-roots groups have a lot of unpaid help. The more money an organization has, the more it can afford to pay." Olsen has found hospitals to be the best-paying nonprofits, social service organizations the worst. Another recruiter, Linda Broessel, agrees with him on hospitals, but thinks arts organizations are the poorest paying, except for the biggest ones. "Top universities pay very well, too," she adds.

Preservation Maryland, one of the nation's oldest private nonprofit statewide historic preservation groups, headquartered in Baltimore, paid its executive director between $25,000 and $30,000 in 1986. Responsibilities, according to a *New York Times* ad, include "cultural and resource management, fiscal and long-range planning, community and legislative relations, and membership development." A bachelor's degree and five years of experience in historical preservation/cultural administration are required; knowledge of architecture, design, and construction are preferred.

Location is an important consideration for two reasons. First, according to Bill Olsen, "Salaries reflect the cost of living in a region. You're paid more in New York City than in

Keokuk, Iowa." Olsen has also learned "some people won't work in a big city; others really want to. Rural life can be a big attraction."

Herb Paris observes, "Maine salaries are lower than [those in] big cities—and so is the cost of living. The quality of life is higher here. You can live in a lovely house on the ocean in Maine, rather than a high-priced condo. Employees come here for a stimulating job and an environmentally attractive area. The key trade-off is you can live outside a metropolitan area somewhat less expensively."

Bryan Knapp moved to nonprofit because he wanted more time for his personal life. The frequent travel required by his previous job meant "keeping in touch with friends by postcard." The university job leaves him more time outside work. While Knapp took a substantial pay cut in his new position, he does not feel deprived in his second postcorporate year and finds that he can live on his university earnings. (In lower-priced times, he had bought a city apartment and a country house.) "There's no bonus now, but no hardship. I have a nice corner office with a park view. I don't have financial planning assistance anymore, but my need for it is less."

Knapp points out that some corporate "perks" can be deceptive. Although American Express paid for his health-club membership, he had to pay steep taxes on it. Now he has joined the university sports center for $175 a year. He appreciates not having to wear suits to work anymore but admits missing the globe-trotting a little.

"Leadership positions are fairly well-paid—not $200,000, but a comfortable wage," Jessica Andrews maintains. "However, there's a huge drop to middle management—fund raising and marketing—so they tend to come and go fairly frequently." Al Milano reports, "Cleveland nonprofits pay about 10 percent below the market rate for staff salaries. When the federal government began to pay its employees market rates, other nonprofits followed suit, after the Johnson years when the administration was really lavish." Herb Paris finds that his hours, salary, and benefits are comparable to those in for-profit health care. Employees in the nonprofit sector rarely complain about benefits, either. Marcus

Laster's benefits are "standard for the industry." He has a national pension plan that travels with him, wherever he works, and includes life and health insurance. In addition, he receives a paid family membership in the congregation, four weeks of vacation, and time to attend professional conferences and meetings.

Chief executives of America's largest foundations, with assets of $100 million or more, earn close to six-figure salaries. Most well-known national nonprofits in the mid 1980s pay their top officials between $50,000 and $100,000. Salaries vary with the geographic location, the type and size of the organization, and its solvency.

"No one ever feels they're getting paid enough," observes Marcus Laster; however, he continues, "the salary level is commensurate with the responsibility level. Most synagogues now pay their professional staff similarly to what they'd earn in private industry. If you want proper personnel, you have to be competitive in the marketplace. At the senior level, someone choosing my profession knows that while they may not be earning a huge amount of money, they'll receive a livable income and reap intangible benefits."

HOW TO BECOME AN EXECUTIVE DIRECTOR

The paths to executive director positions are quite diverse. While no particular education or training is required for most such positions, hospital and educational administrators are generally required to have the appropriate master's degree. An M.B.A., M.P.A., or other advanced degree will undoubtedly become more common. How, then, do nonprofit leaders move towards their success? Invaribly, the answer is a combination of hard work, dedication to their employers and to the cause in general, and results. Most of these executives move to the top spot at a new organization by three methods: being scouted by an executive recruiter, hearing of a promising opening through their own network of acquaintances, or replying to an ad in a professional publication or local newspaper.

Herb Paris, who has been in Maine since 1978, has an M.H.A. from the Medical College of Virginia and 25 years of experience. He was teaching at Yale and working at a 1,000-bed New Haven hospital when the Brunswick Regional Hospital recruited him through its network of contacts.

While working in the development office of a major library for two-and-a-half years, Al Milano increased annual contributions from $1.1 to $3.5 million. The donor base grew from 2,500 to 45,000, but his advancement path was blocked. "I decided to have more fun, and looked for a spot in the performing arts with the idea it might be more enjoyable. I answered a journal ad for the Dallas Symphony Orchestra." In his five years there, starting at $32,000, he was promoted to managing director, responsible for fund raising and producing all nonclassical musical events. After conflicts with the board, he called the Dallas Theater Center, having heard of an opening through the "cultural grapevine." He was hired as general manager, before moving to Cleveland in 1984. Milano has a B.A. in political science, and one semester of graduate work in the same field.

Bob Ohlerking has a degree in urban planning and was with the Public Development Corporation before shifting to his present post directing an off-shoot of his county's chamber of commerce. His work with retail merchants all over the county, and with 40 commercial streets downtown in particular, made him the likeliest candidate for the downtown-development job.

Bryan Knapp found his position in the education section of his city's newspaper. He has a master's degree and has completed everything but the dissertation for his doctorate in industrial psychology. "I was seeking more broad-based work. Responsible for 11,000 employees, I wondered, how many ways can you run a personnel department? I could only get hired for the same job elsewhere. It was time for a new challenge." The university possibility struck him because he had enjoyed adjunct professor and senior advisor roles at the University of Minnesota and the State University of New York at Buffalo. "My interests were really in marketing and product development. I had to know those features for human resources planning. This has not been a big change in terms of duties," he reflects. Knapp hasn't changed his weekday hours much, either, still putting in ten-hour days most of the time, but he no longer has to bring work home. He takes an hour out for the university sports center each morning and visits his program directors frequently. Knapp brings his profit-sector awareness to the nonprofit world, commenting ruefully that "the staff has little awareness of customer service. Ours is a premium-priced product, competitive in the marketplace—so at least be courteous on the phone! Nonprofits need to understand the clients. Our product is more than just the delivery of a class."

Jessica Andrews ended up in theater somewhat accidentally. Her father was an actor and director, her mother a dancer, so Andrews had participated in theatrical productions from an early age. When she reentered the job market after taking time out for children, it was thus natural for her to gravitate back to theater. She took an administrative assistant position with the Hartford Stage Company, where she had done some summer work.

> The pay was low, and the tasks new. My upbringing allowed me to see that everyone pitches in and helps to get things done. I had a very open attitude, knowing that people would help me. Theater is very supportive. I'm willing to say I don't know something, so I can learn. Twenty years ago, Hartford was in a growth stage. Soon after I started, an assistant business manager line was created, and I got it. Several other promotions led to the managing director job. I've always been on the management side, but never isolated from what happens on the stage.

After ten years, she moved to Rochester for four years, running a smaller company until it was time to step back. She then joined an arts management consulting group and worked with people all over the country for five years. While she was glad to be relieved of the day-to-day responsibility for an organization's fate, Andrews was loathe to leave the business. She maintained links with other arts administrators, because, she states, "your connections become your support system," and she kept reevaluating her readiness to return to a theater. In the spring of 1985, weary of traveling, Andrews found that "I missed the producing side and began serious discussion with several theaters. Back into the fray!" As managing director of the Indianapolis Repertory Theatre, she now works many evenings, often until 11 P.M., "to have contact with the actors. The reason I'm here is *because* of the actors. You can't keep those hours regularly, yet theater is an evening business and you need to be there as manager."

Another path to executive director jobs is to found the organization, out of deep personal involvement and commitment to the cause. Advocates for the homeless in Philadelphia established a self-help training program, headed by Chris Sprowal, formerly homeless himself. After training local participants, the group, called the Committee For Dignity And Fairness For The Homeless, hopes to send organizers to other cities with large homeless populations needing assistance. The Peoples Firehouse, which describes itself as "a community-based, neighborhood organization," grew out of a successful community effort to stop the city and the fire department from closing a local engine company in 1975. After three years of research and negotiations, the group succeeded in persuading the city. The Peoples Firehouse was incorporated in late 1977, and its first formal funding, from the Comprehensive Employment and Training Act (CETA), allowed for six community organizers and a project director, Fred Ringler. Ringler reports, "As a direct result of this successful community organizing effort, the Peoples Firehouse committed itself to preserving and restoring vital city services in [the community], and to [achieving] goals and objectives in a number of areas of concern to the residential, commercial, and industrial sectors. These include housing, arson/fire prevention, commercial revitalization, economic and industrial development." Today, Ringler is executive director of an

80-person staff, with a budget nearing $3 million. He travels all over the country advising other groups on setting up comparable programs. In 1986, he secured $250,000 from the U.S. Fire Administration for the largest single demonstration project around life-saving issues.

Marian Wright Edelman founded the Children's Defense Fund in 1973, after directing the NAACP Legal Defense and Education Fund office in Jackson, Mississippi, and working as a congressional liaison in Washington for the Southern Christian Leadership Conference. She and her staff of 70 operate with an annual budget of $4.6 million as advocates for 61 million children on welfare, health, juvenile justice, and family-related topics. A Yale Law School graduate, Mrs. Edelman is directly involved in lobbying Congress and federal agencies for better laws, regulations, and programs affecting children. She goes to court on occasion, too.

Where can you go once you have reached the top of a nonprofit organization? The most frequent step is to the leadership post at a larger or more prestigious nonprofit, where earnings will often be higher and impact greater. As Herb Paris indicated, location can also be a selection factor when you choose a new position. Some nonprofit executives move to government or foundation posts, so they can be on the giving rather than the receiving end. Another path is to become a consultant for a profit-making corporation providing management or fund-raising expertise to nonprofit clients for a fee. Such consulting jobs often require a good deal of travel but can be lucrative, varied, and interesting.

For anyone considering a nonprofit position, and particularly for an executive director who will assume major responsibilities, take the time to do a little research. "Evaluate a not-for-profit by the latest financial figures, their annual report, and the National Charities Information Bureau," recommends Linda Broessel. "Changing federal and state regulations affect nonprofits a lot. Find out how old and how large the organization's deficit is."

During his interviews, Al Milano learned the Cleveland

Play House was $5 million in debt, but, he reasons, "that's not necessarily a reason to decline the job. It turned out they had hired Philip Johnson to design their theater, incurring the deficit, which I felt would be eradicated." His first year was tough, but the situation is improving now. Milano's real challenge was changing "virtually every administrative department head. Now they're all under 40, and I plan to train them in whatever they lack," Milano reports.

The Development Office

INTRODUCTION

The development office is not only unique to nonprofits, but is essential to their continued existence. This is the department that raises the money to support the organization's daily and long-term activities, pay salaries, finance new programs or buildings, and do all the other things that allow a not-for- profit to carry out its mission.

Development is widely perceived as the main growth area in the nonprofit sphere today. Deep government cutbacks in funding have forced organizations to cultivate their own sources, just as the advent of compact, easy-to-use, inexpensive microcomputers is streamlining donor record keeping and direct-mail activities even for small agencies. As the development office gains more impact and importance within its organization, salaries, titles, and power grow.

"Fund raising is the land of opportunity," exclaims Jack Rimalover, vice president for resource development and public relations at a prominent urban hospital. "The field didn't exist this strongly or importantly ten years ago. Its corporate counterpart is sales, marketing, advertising, or promotion." Rimalover should know; before joining his hospital 11 years ago, he was vice president for marketing at Creative Playthings, then the largest educational-toy company in America.

FUNCTIONS OF THE DEVELOPMENT OFFICE

When fund raising is suggested as a career possibility, the most frequent response is "Oh, I could never do that. I can't ask people for money all the time." The second likeliest reply is, "Are they the people who put those tin cans in restaurants?" Both of these popular notions are misrepresentations of the field. In 1985 contributions to America's 300,000 nonprofit organizations totaled $79.8 billion, so it is clear that fund raising has gone beyond the familiar collection canisters displayed in neighborhood stores. In fact, very little of a development professional's time is spent asking people for money. So what is it that fund raisers are paid to do all day?

A well-run, effective development office is involved in a wide set of activities. In many small organizations, the "office" consists of one full-time staff member, who tries to allocate the time as efficiently as possible. In a new nonprofit, the executive director is generally the fund raiser, too. Taking into account the time or staff available, these are usual tasks a development office will perform:

- Plan fund-raising events.
- Recruit, train, and monitor volunteers.
- Devise and maintain effective donor records.
- Prepare mailings.
- Maintain contact with board members.
- Interact with the rest of the organization, including the executive director, and the accounting, public relations, publications, and membership staffs.

- Identify, research, and cultivate prospective major donors.
- Research, write proposals to, and visit foundations, government agencies, and corporations.
- Acknowledge gifts; maintain contact with donors.
- Meet with current grantmakers regularly; submit reports as required.
- Screen and hire consultants (if necessary).
- Solicit in-kind contributions (gifts that are not cash).
- Plan fund-raising campaigns and schedules of gifts.
- Help develop promotion and publicity materials.
- Manage property that has been given to the nonprofit.
- Solicit deferred gifts.
- Manage, hire, and supervise the staff (development director).

QUALIFICATIONS AND TRAINING FOR THE DEVELOPMENT OFFICE

How does one learn to do all those things? Fund raising has traditionally been an on-the-job training field, receptive to people from assorted backgrounds and appealing to those with a range of skills. Few formal training programs exist today (Vanderbilt University and the New School have master's programs; New York University, the Fund-raising School, and the Grantsmanship Center offer continuing education courses), and a graduate degree is hardly a necessity for entering the profession. So what *do* you need to get a first job in development?

"If you didn't know what to do with your liberal arts degree, fund raising is for you," says Margaret Holman, development director of the American Academy of Dramatic Arts. She looks for "bright, articulate, quick learners, who can write and roll with the punches" to work on her staff.

Burr Gibson, a fund raiser for nearly 40 years and now chairman of the consulting firm Marts & Lundy, suggests, "Gray hair and hemorrhoids may be the two traits a fund raiser needs most: the gray hair gives you distinction, the hemorrhoids a look of concern." On a more serious note,

Gibson describes some of the contrasting qualities a development professional needs, including "creativity combined with attention to detail and an analytic approach."

"You'll have to be a good communicator, both oral and written, as well as a good listener. You have to plan and execute a program, which means you can't stop at a successful planning stage. A fund raiser takes care of both people and paperwork. You'll need to be aggressive and occasionally cautious."

Jim Meeuwsen, the New York Zoological Society's director of public affairs, looks for "writing skills, presence and confidence, articulateness, research, some initiative, and curiosity. You learn some things, but the innate qualities have to be there: organizational ability, concern for the world and people, the ability to make a commitment."

"I look for someone who will do a little more, who has an inner motor," says Karen Szurek. "My staff have to be intelligent, able to deal with the public, other staff, and each other. Temperament is important—no histrionics! People have to be careful with detail and care about the quality of their work."

At Catholic Relief Services, the Director of Donor Services, Anne Smith, recently hired a new assistant whose previous job was with a commercial radio station in Florida. Smith insists, "The staff must be committed to Catholic Relief Services' efforts, not just to fund raising. You must be more than a 9-to-5-er, and enjoy variety. Fund raising takes discipline and strategy, plus enthusiasm. You have to see the challenge, set realistic goals, and follow up on calls." Besides communication skills, she finds computer literacy important; her department's direct mail program sends six appeals a year to 200,000 people.

Jack Rimalover points out that, "as with any job, you have to start out with routine scut work. I look for a self-starter, with initiative and a track record. You must be an actor. Tolerance, patience, and a thick skin are additional needs. This is the same ball game as corporate marketing or advertising." Rimalover's advice is to "do anything to get a foot in the door. For your job hunt, be sure to follow up. Keep in touch. Send thank-you notes. Spelling counts." He advocates networking. (So do we, as you will learn in Chapter 11.) The fund-raising jobs at his hospital start at clerk-typist, and include data entry, accounts posting, gift acknowledgments (some form of thank-you letters), and receipts. The next level is supervisory, including research on corporations and foundations which may have an interest in the work of his organization, special events, direct mail, and research on other categories of donor.

Rimalover considers special events an expanding segment of fund raising, as more organizations try to raise money via testimonial dinners, film premiers, cocktail parties, or other benefit activities. He has found this approach to be so effective for his hospital that he has added a full-time special events staff member.

Now managing director of the Cleveland Play House, Al Milano started his career in fund raising. He was a grant director for government contracts at the National Welfare Rights Organization in the late 1960s, setting up seminars all over the country. This led to a fund-raising trainee spot at the National Council on Crime and Delinquency (NCCD), paying $11,000. "My boss was a former Presbyterian minister, and the training consisted of arranging fund-raising appointments. He told me to put a mirror behind a phone. He said, 'Make sure you're smiling when you're trying to set up appointments.' The second month, the directors told me, 'Now you're a senior fund raiser. Go out and ask for gifts.' " Given 200 qualified leads, Milano arranged 50 appointments for a two-week trip to Pittsburgh, returning with $16,000 in corporate gifts. In three-and-a-half years of corporate fund raising for NCCD, he saw CEOs all over America. "I was trained to look a guy in the eye, tell the story, and ask for a gift. My two bosses taught me every trick in the book. I had a ball." His salary had increased by more than a third by the time Milano decided to leave because he could not learn anything new anymore.

"Development is problem solving," asserts Michael Jones, development director at a National Public Radio station. "In a good organization, the needs are easily and clearly defined, and so are the development directors's goals. The people element is a plus. I like setting up organizational tasks to get the job done." Jones has also worked for the USO and several other nonprofits in five states. He began his fundraising career as a canvasser for the Coalition for Consumer Activism in Providence and Fair Share in Boston, two neighborhood projects using statewide issues to organize local communities. Jones found canvassing for contributions an interesting training ground. "You had to shift your rap in ten seconds. After a year and a half of door-to-door, I can sell anything." When his former wife accepted a job in Michigan, where the unemployment rate was then 28 percent, Jones moved there and raised $30,000 in a community of 100,000 residents. He answered a local newspaper ad to get his three-day-a-week job with the Cystic Fibrosis Foundation.

From his diverse experiences, Jones observes, "it's easier to get those lower-paying jobs. Small organizations are very good starting places, because you'll see the basic not-for-profit functions. A small organization has all generalists, and no specialists. Being a generalist is the best learning experience."

Steve Bajardi looks for media, public relations, or communications skills in his staff. For his first nonprofit position when he left banking, he started the development office at Juvenile Diabetes Foundation International and built it up to an annual budget of $985,000. When he left six-and-a-half years later, he had a staff of 15. Traveling frequently to visit some of the 150 chapters across America, Bajardi worked 70-hour weeks for a stretch of time before he was made director of development. He casts a serious perspective on the work. "To use donor dollars, you must be more moral, more ethical, more responsible than anywhere else. Few are there to remind you about the bottom line. The concern is more for human need than for profit." When he hires, Bajardi concedes, "personal rapport and the chemistry of the interview count for 90 percent." He screens out frequent job changers or people with unclear track records, seeking resumes "that are candid and well done, without sloppiness or misspellings to suggest carelessness." He avoids people with large gaps in their employment past, and looks for "eagerness, high energy, enthusiasm for life in general, confidence, willingness to do something extra to get the job done."

FUND RAISING AS A JOB

Starting salaries in this area, of course, are relatively modest. Linda Broessel, a national recruiter of nonprofit executives, remarks, "Nonprofits pay in satisfaction; no one gets rich in these fields." To Margaret Holman, "Fund raisers are not as much dollar-oriented as issue-oriented." Confirming Holman's comment, half the fund raisers we interviewed had changed careers to enter the field, often at a substantial reduction in pay. What are the rewards of this expanding profession?

Rewards

For Maryann Alfano, at the International Center for the Disabled, "it's the first time in my life I can say I love what I'm doing." After ten years as a manager at an apparel sales company, she did volunteer work at a local hospital for a year, before finding her current spot as director of corporate and foundation gifts. "At my sales company, there were nice people and a nice atmosphere—and that corporate mentality. In the nonprofit sector [there] is more camaraderie. . . . We all knock ourselves out for the same reason. If my colleague gets a big check from an individual donor, I'm happy for her." Much of Alfano's time is spent researching and visiting foundations or local companies that may be willing to give her organization a gift.

Lynne Hayden left a 13-year career in advertising sales to become a development assistant at an urban community college. She appreciates "working for a place I believe in, that I think provides a unique service and does it well. There's a reason to work hard for it. If I were less happy with the nature of the organization, I'd like the job less." Hayden took a 50 percent pay cut to enter her new field, but has a long list of the job's rewards including "the unlimited opportunity to be creative, especially in a new situation. I have an open-minded boss, and the chance to do things I've never done before, like our first black-tie dinner." She also cites flexibility and getting results as positive features of her new position.

Over and over, development professionals mention diversity, challenge, and fun as the joys of the job. Karen Szurek, Museum of Broadcasting development director, likes being a "people broker":

> As development director, I'm involved in almost everything, and I sit in on all decisions. The work is fun; I get to see lots of interesting people. The "glamour" is in meeting all sectors of the community, finding out a lot about who's connected to who, and what makes the world tick. I'm always learning something fascinating. You see a lot more [in development work] than you might selling computers.

"Because mine is a small organization, I make the decisions," Margaret Holman notes. She has only two bosses at her current job, and is out of her office more than she is in it. "You become more specialized in a large organization," she finds.

Steve Bajardi is the first full-time development director at the Princess Grace Foundation. He has a staff of two and an annual operating budget of $200,000. His weekend-long annual gala for the foundation raised $1.3 million for the organization, which awards grants to young performing artists. Before shifting to fund raising, Bajardi was a data-processing manager for a large bank. "I'm dealing with a whole new class of people now—the super affluent," he finds. "Their motivations are different. I've met Frank Sinatra, Jimmy Stewart, real movers and shakers." In addition to the usual management tasks, Bajardi is responsible for writing, public speaking, direct mail, special events, and corporate solicitation. He finds the diversity of his job exciting.

During our interview with Jack Rimalover, a prominent local restauranteur and board member of the hospital dropped by to present him with a generous check. "This is part of the fun of the job," Rimalover said, grinning to his visitors. Indeed, receiving the gifts is not only enjoyable—it's one of the ways a fund raiser's effectiveness is finally measured. The considerations include how many gifts have been received, from how many donors, and for how much money.

Drawbacks

As with any type of nonprofit work, of course, fund raising is not for everyone. Over and over, development professionals emphasize that you must care about the cause and welcome challenge. Hours can be long, because of board meetings, special events during the evening, or in response to deadlines. "With all this work to do, you feel so guilty if you take a day off. The lack of support staff makes planning more limited," notes Lynne Hayden. Michael Jones works for nine days straight during the three on-air fund raisers his radio station conducts each year, and he goes to a fair number of weekend events, too. While he does not work from 9 A.M. to 5 P.M., he does work more than 40 hours a week. "The schedule is flexible; I can take time off when it's slow. Last summer, I took a month off for vacation." Anne Smith does not work weekends, but says hers is the equivalent of a six-day week. "Everyone's still there at 6 P.M. and my secretary often comes in on Saturdays. I take work home. We all try to handle the endless chain of emergencies."

At the Museum of Broadcasting, Karen Szurek first gives the official hours, 9:15 A.M. to 5:15 P.M. then remarks, "rarely does anyone leave before 6. The staff may come in on Saturday, or take work home. I spend some evenings going to museum-related events." Jim Meeuwsen, at the Zoological Society, works a 50-hour week because of the special programs to increase membership, like Elephant Weekend. Some evenings are devoted to special programs for members or trustees; others include lectures or other activities Meeuwsen or a staff member attends.

The National Council on Alcoholism's development

officer, Lisa Leinbach, usually comes in earlier than her 9:15 A.M. to 5:15 P.M. schedule dictates, but tries to leave with coworkers to avoid being the last person around. At his hospital, Jack Rimalover finds the hours "roughly 9 to 5 on the administrative side. The medical staff have different schedules." These days, Steve Bajardi at the Princess Grace Foundation claims a general 9-to-5 schedule. However, he meets his boss for dinner once a week and stays until 7 P.M. on two evenings. His assistant often stays past 5 P.M. as well.

Because most people in development stress commitment and flexibility as essential for success, expect to put in more than 40 hours a week on the average. Fund raising is not for you if you want the kind of job you can walk out on at 5 P.M. "To be good," says recruiter Linda Broessel, "you probably take the job home with you. In arts organizations, the development director attends nearly every performance, plus dress rehearsals that donors are invited to. The development director has to remain calm under pressure, so you need a release." Recommending sports as an outlet, Linda comments, "there's no more Lady Bountiful; even Brooke Astor works. Don't choose this field because you're lazy."

Satisfied fund raisers are matter-of-fact about the hours, because the organization's work is so important to them. Ed Shanken, director of resource development at the National Foundation for Ileitis and Colitis, explains his feeling that "maybe *this* researcher will find a cure for these 2 million people. That's what drives you."

Aside from the long hours, are there any other drawbacks to fund raising? "Space limitations," moans Anne Smith. "Our organization is growing, but the building isn't. We could hire more staff, but there's no place to put them. Our equipment could be updated, too." Michael Jones cites the "frustrations of undercapitalization. Being a good manager, I know what I could do *if*. . . .The physical surroundings are unattractive at my radio station. And I know I'm worth more than I'm being paid." His current earnings are just under $30,000.

For Lynne Hayden, the disadvantage is "we're generalists.

I have very little experience in any single aspect of fund raising." She also states, "We get lots of vacation days, but who has the time to take them, or the money to go anywhere? It's frustrating." Hayden notes that fund raisers enjoy working hard and don't mind being out of the limelight, since this is background work.

A degree of pressure is built into the responsibilities, too, because a nonprofit depends on its development office to bring in the funds to support the staff's work and programs, as well as new gifts or grants for expanded activities. Development professionals have to learn when to say no to unreasonable or unrealistic requests from coworkers.

A large percentage of development workers are women. Does this mean it's a good field for females? "Oh, yes," asserts Maryann Alfano. "But all the vice presidents are still men. It's a good field for mature women. In the corporate world, you're over the hill past 35." Judy Luken, executive director of The Caring Community, a senior citizens' program, disagrees. "In fund raising, as in the rest of society, women are paid less than men. The 'old boys' network' prevails here: fund raising is still a white male profession, for the middle aged and middle class." She does concede, though, that women are moving up faster than they had been.

Specialties in Fund Raising

The best way to insure advancement in fund raising, whether you're male or female, would be to gain experience or know-how in one of the fast-growing specialties: planned giving, marketing, or direct mail. Planned giving focuses on securing deferred gifts for your organization from people who agree to include your nonprofit among their bequests. This is a complex, expanding area involving legal and accounting factors. All reasonably sophisticated nonprofits are launching or expanding a planned giving program to interest prospective donors in considering a long-range gift.

Marketing is not specifically a fund-raising function but is closely related to it. Marketing specialists at a nonprofit are involved in attracting consumers to the services of the organization, like the classes at a college or community center. Universities, in fact, openly discuss marketing methods for luring new undergraduates in an era of dwindling high-school populations. Other categories of nonprofits are beginning to explore licensing of their name or products as a possible means for generating revenues that can be applied to operating expenses. The CARE Bears are one such arrangement. Until very recently, the concept of marketing was anathema in most nonprofit circles; it was regarded as the crass, money-hungry mentality prevalent in business circles but blissfully absent in the not-for-profit sector. Because competition for donor dollars has heightened and inflation drives operating costs continually higher, even the not-for-profit sector is beginning to acknowledge the necessity for more aggressively marketing what they have to offer to the public.

Direct mail is a marketing tool that has proliferated in the 1980s, and with which you are doubtless confronted all the time. Catalogs from Sears, Spiegel, or Saks Fifth Avenue, for example, are direct-mail efforts, designed to encourage you to order items just from reading the material. The nonprofit counterpart, the appeal letter, gives you information about an organization in the hope you will be motivated enough to put a check in the conveniently enclosed envelope, or mark off a membership category on the prestamped postcard so you can be billed later. Norman Lind, who has worked on nonprofits' direct mail for 25 years, enthuses, "You keep creating all day. One person can write to millions. You come up with new ideas, write copy, learn about printing and production, and postal regulations. You're really putting together strategy, packaging, and even record keeping. There are spending controls, because the organization probably operates on a pretty tight budget. We're trying to earn a 'profit' whether we call it that or not." Lind, a former public relations writer for the brokerage industry, adds that learning to use a computer is essential for direct mail. The effectiveness of a direct-mail campaign will be measured, at its completion, by the percentage of responses, the average amount of total giving, and the cost of generating a gift. Writing skills, good organizational ability, and attention to detail are the hallmarks of a direct-mail specialist. Salaries are rising in this capacity, as the need grows.

Career Development

Each category of nonprofits has its own group for fundraising professionals. The largest association, the National Society of Fund-Raising Executives, conducts national and regional conferences and workshops, and has local chapters in major cities. They provide the Certified Fund-Raising Executive (CFRE) designation, which requires five years of experience in the field. Awarded after passing a 200-item multiple-choice exam, the CFRE title is also based on the recipient's service to the profession and actual dollars raised. Executive recruiter Linda Broessel feels the CFRE title can help in a high-level job hunt. The prevailing view in the industry is that the CFRE is a respectable credential and worth acquiring.

However, since you will not be eligible for the CFRE until you have been in the field for a while, what can you do now? If a college or community group nearby offers one, take a course in basic fund-raising techniques to learn the vocabulary and general principles. At the very least, read a few reference books to become familiar with the basic concepts involved. If you are planning on graduate school, Al Milano recommends the arts management program at Yale, and the combined M.B.A./M.F.A. at Southern Methodist University. Lisa Leinbach received an M.B.A. in arts administration from the State University of New York at Binghamton. Try to find a graduate business or public administration program that offers courses concentrating on nonprofit management.

To start out in fund raising, though, graduate school really isn't necessary. The profession has been wide open to diverse backgrounds and has attracted numerous former clergymen and performing artists, among others. The fund raisers we interviewed have undergraduate degrees in natural resources, political science, art history, sociology, theater, and all of the other liberal arts, plus graduate degrees (if any) in business or international affairs. Rather than education, successful fund raisers share a commitment to the cause for which they work and an appreciation for being part of their chosen organization.

6

The Program Department

Providing the Service

INTRODUCTION

All nonprofits provide some sort of benefit to the public, so some part of each organization is involved in actually delivering the service. The range of service providers is as wide and varied as the universe of nonprofits; it includes social workers, librarians, nurses, teachers, professors, community organizers, lawyers helping to solve the problems of the needy, counselors, zoo keepers, and many more. Entire volumes have been written on each of these career areas, so we will not attempt to tackle each one in depth. Instead, we would like to convey a sense of the rewards and difficulties of a number of different, representative service jobs in widely divergent types of organizations.

ATTORNEY FOR A NONPROFIT ORGANIZATION

Tim Jensen was hired at Volunteer Lawyers for the Arts right from law school, after a stint at the Public Education

Association. In describing the deep rewards his work provides, Jensen comments that "you can make a living and keep your ideals. It's fun. You enjoy what you're doing." He also cites the gratification of such projects as getting tax status for a dance company. "If I worked for a big law firm, and one oil company was suing another, it [would be] an intellectual satisfaction: you work for people with money, and do a job well. In nonprofit, you work for people who have nowhere else to go. We have much more human contact." He admits, however, that the work never really ends.

> Someone else always needs help. Even if you have too much work, it's hard to turn down someone who can't get other help. . . .In a corporation, you might work hard to get more money or a promotion—personal advancement. In nonprofit, you don't advance yourself; it's not an individualized activity. You feel pressure to keep giving as much as you possibly can, so you must learn to set limits for yourself. . . .If you don't control it, you'll burn out.

However, Jenson also remarks, in a nonprofit organization, "you get reinforcement for doing more, because people say thank you." He appreciates the positive feedback his work provides.

Comparing his legal activities to those in a typical firm, he points out "at a big law firm, it could be five years before you see a client. At a nonprofit, with less supervision available, they can't afford to do that; they need you to be productive as soon as you're hired." For those considering a legal specialization in a nonprofit area, Jensen warns of the shrinking opportunities in not-for-profit law and the need to be a self-starter. He acknowledges the potential insecurity about the profession and cautions "don't pick nonprofit to learn more about the profession—*care* about the cause."

Jensen's duties include arguing with galleries, clients, publishers, and record companies who hire artists. He often gives talks to groups of professional or undergraduate artists about their legal rights and the best ways to protect themselves from mistreatment or exploitation. For aspiring nonprofit attorneys, he recommends "work one summer at a big law firm. Often, law students work pro bono for nonprofits, which helps them get a job in nonprofit, but it might be better...to learn at a big law firm." Jensen also cautions, "nonprofits don't recruit; they can't afford to send staff out to campuses, and they place smaller ads. The human network is critically important."

Lisa Tessler, the placement counselor at a top law school, says of attorney positions in nonprofit organizations, "they do exist, but are increasingly more difficult to obtain." Her law school has a disproportionate number of graduates entering public service—about 13 percent, most of whom begin their careers with legal aid or legal services organizations. Generally, more positions are available doing prosecution and criminal defense work than civil. While the job market is tight, Tessler points out that opportunities exist in urban and rural areas throughout the country. Some law schools offer loan repayment assistance programs to graduates starting public interest careers, whose relatively low salaries make it difficult to pay back loans of $30,000 or more.

In this highly competitive specialty, with opportunities shrinking, Tessler notes that the major employers include district attorney and public defender offices, legal aid and legal services organizations, departments of law in major cities, and federal government agencies. Attorney General and U.S. Attorney's offices typically hire law graduates with a minimum of two years' experience. She recommends *Community Jobs*, *The Public Interest Clearinghouse Employment Report*, The National Legal Aid and Defender Association (NLADA)'s *Cornerstone*, and the *National and Federal Legal Employment Report* as publications providing useful job leads.

SOCIAL WORKER AT A HOSPITAL

Gail Martino left her previous career in finance to attend graduate school in social work. She found her job, at a large municipal hospital, through a local newspaper ad. Even though she went on 40 or 50 interviews, she found job hunting in this field easier than the corporate counterpart had been. According to Martino, "After a brief meeting, an interviewer would say, 'When can you start?' "

Martino is part of a treatment team at a teaching hospital, where patients can stay for up to two months. Although the physician makes the ultimate decisions, she says "I'm an advocate. I look beyond what the patient needs medically to consider if the patient can return to work. Is the living condition viable?" Martino does crisis, or short-term, family therapy, and she enjoys it because

> I'm very active and vocal. In crisis work, I can make something happen sooner. It's very challenging. You have to think fast, as someone is telling you something, about what to say next, and create a treatment plan. When I really feel an intervention has been useful and has changed a family's pattern, it's much more satisfying than putting a good budget together. I feel I'm growing psychologically, understanding myself better.

While the hospital's professional staff usually works a 40-hour week, Martino stays longer and attends conferences to learn more. Her immediate supervisor, the chief of inpatient services, gives one hour each week of individual supervision and a weekly 90-minute family therapy seminar.

Martino's favorite part of the job is "the surprises—the family secrets that come up. There are issues of confidentiality: do I have to tell the lover of an AIDS patient about the illness? It's challenging intellectually and emotionally."

Of her path to social work, Martino reflects, "my self-image was very tied to a business identity. Little things, like dressing a certain way, or having a secretary to get my eat-in lunch, became part of the identity." She started her career change at age 38, after contemplating it for several years and participating in career-change workshops. The first step was a second master's degree. The second was quitting her highly paid job. "I had all the frills, and it was hard to give them up. It's difficult being an old fledgling. I now work for bosses who are younger than I am." On the positive side, she finds, "I think I get more respect from colleagues because I am older; being valued as a mature person may have helped me get a good job."

Pleased with and committed to her new profession—despite earning about one-third of her former budget director salary—Martino reports, "my goals are much more focused and directed because of my age. I want to start a private practice, as a therapist, in a year or two."

Social workers and counselors help people solve problems or make adjustments to difficult situations. They may work in schools, hospitals, community agencies, nursing homes, or residences for special populations. We met one woman whose employer, a large funeral home, paid her to obtain an M.S.W. degree to help her handle grieving families with greater sensitivity and skill. A graduate degree is not always required but is advantageous in terms of both earnings and level of responsibility.

A master's degree in social work, generally requiring about 60 graduate credits, or a master's degree in counseling, 36 credits and up, are the professional credentials in this discipline. Starting salaries are usually in the high teens to low twenties. With advancement, of course, comes more money and more supervisory responsibility. Counselors with an M.S.W. degree and three years of experience, for example, can expect to earn about $25,000.

A representative job at a state-run psychiatric hospital in mid 1986 as a primary therapist for emotionally disturbed adolescents required two years experience and Spanish-language fluency, and offered up to $26,500. Volunteers of America, recruiting for its homeless men's shelter, sought social workers familiar with mental illness, substance abuse, alcoholism, and housing issues. Salary would be about $25,000, with an M.S.W. and three years of experience.

Positions requiring only a B.A. degree, such as counseling homeless men or assisting in employment placement and making referrals to educational, vocational, or training programs, generally pay $19,000 or more. A typical job (as described in a *New York Times*) in "a rapidly expanding community mental health residence...includes intake screening, crisis intervention, staff training, and development of new programs." Seeking a year's experience plus "strong clinical, communication, and research skills," this employer would pay $18,000 or more for a social worker. An unusual post (also advertised in the *New York Times*) calling for an M.S.W. degree was "Director of Singles Dating Service in a large city." With a negotiable salary, the director would supervise staff, coordinate the program of interviewing and matching singles, work in public relations and advertising for the service, and deal with the board and advisory committee.

Most social work jobs are more conventional than that one. Good opportunities today involve geriatric care, alcohol and drug abuse counseling, and hospital positions. Of course, no one chooses social work for the money, but many professionals do supplement their incomes through a private practice. The Certified Social Worker designation (C.S.W.) makes a person with an M.S.W. eligible for third-party payments from insurance providers, so a private practice is a realistic option. Social workers can specialize in marriage or family counseling, sexual problems, substance abuse, individual or group psychotherapy, or any other area for which their training and experience has prepared them. In private practice, social workers operate much as psychologists do; because an M.S.W. takes much less time to obtain than a Ph.D. in psychology, a person with an M.S.W. typically charges lower fees than his or her counterpart with a doctorate.

LIBRARIAN IN A SPECIALTY AREA

"Many people choose librarianship as a second career," observes Candace Kuhta, coordinator of public services at the Foundation Center. "It's a very profitable profession. You can take the skills anywhere, and learn a new job. It covers a broad range of interests, and you're always learning new subjects, so you can help the public better."

With a degree in English literature and varied work experience, Kuhta went to library school in Wales, hoping to specialize in rare books. With her new master's degree in librarianship, she quickly discovered she had selected a very narrow field. After one year in the rare book room at Brentano's, she became an editorial assistant for a publisher of book auction records, editing catalog entries. For her next career move, she spent a year as a librarian at a historical society, working with "old photos and lots of local history." She came to the Foundation Center, a well-known national nonprofit clearinghouse and resource center for other nonprofit organizations, three and a half years ago. Kuhta finds that the job combines many of her interests, which include the arts and history. "It's quite a learning experience. A special library lets you learn a subject you might not know otherwise. You get a chance to teach, by orienting the patrons who visit academic or special libraries. If you're a book fanatic, it's fun to be around them all the time." She enjoys group work and dealing with people in general, and thus finds the many presentations she gives at the Foundation Center rewarding. However, she notes that the "technical services (classifying, cataloging, researching) are behind the scenes, so if you're not a people person, this is a good path."

What skills does librarianship require? "Communication is important," Kuhta asserts, meaning both speaking and writing. "Memos and reports are generated by each of our libraries. You may write articles, introductions to bibliographies, and papers. Sometimes you have to convince management of the need for more staff, or money for something in particular. You may write reports, review books, or—at the Foundation Center—prepare training materials. Verbal skills are crucial."

Kuhta divides libraries into three broad categories: academic, public, and special, which includes corporate libraries. Academic libraries serve the students and faculty of a specific institution and can cover a vast spectrum of information topics. Public libraries, funded by local communities and state governments for their residents, offer books, periodicals, and materials of general interest. A business library is usually located within a corporation's headquarters and keeps materials relevant to the company's field of endeavor. Special libraries, such as the Academy of Medicine, deal only with a particular topic. Public and academic libraries are often open evenings and weekends, but the hours at the Foundation Center are mostly 9 A.M. to 5 P.M. Monday through Friday. The Foundation Center is open late one evening and keeps only one (rotating) staff member on hand, but most of the staff actually works more than 40 hours a week.

Contrary to its image, librarianship is hectic, Kuhta reports. "The Foundation Center and the university library where my husband works both require constant public contact. On the technical services side, the workload is heavy. Organizations can't hire enough staff for everything that's needed." Every Foundation Center librarian puts in some hours at the reference desk, and all share the public-speaking requirements. Because they receive a lot of telephone inquiries from member organizations of the Foundation Center, two librarians are needed at the reference desk during daytime hours. In addition, each librarian has a specialty responsibility, such as acquisitions or cataloging.

When hiring, Kuhta looks for "a little experience, and all the standard library skills." She has hired former teachers and publishers among others, and considers public speaking essential. "You must enjoy public contact, be outgoing and willing to give service. You have to stay up to date on philanthropy and librarianship. It's not a behind-the-scenes job. The pace is rather hectic, with lots of personal service required." The starting salary is about $18,000 to $20,000.

It was hard for Kuhta to think of any disadvantage to her job, because she likes librarianship so much. She cited some problems generally prevalent in the field though. "There aren't many good jobs around, the pay is low yet demands may be very high. Employers may seek a foreign language or second graduate degree, or you may have to publish." Special libraries, such as legal libraries, are the best-paying category, but it is difficult to earn more than $40,000 as a librarian, and typical salaries range from the high teens to the mid twenties. She also notes that if you do not want to move into management, you're stuck. "Librarianship has a poor image. Traditionally a women's field, it has always offered low pay. With today's information explosion, demands are growing on people in the field, but few openings exist. Good automated systems training is relatively in demand, if you can write programs, or manage databases. Low demand has led to some library schools closing."

An M.L.S. degree is a standard requirement for information brokers, with salaries across the country reflecting those Kuhta cited. University and business libraries pay more than public libraries, but may require more experience. For those with training in a subject area, some sophisticated specialty jobs exist, such as slide librarian in a fine arts library. Such a position can require a master's degree in art in addition to the M.L.S., plus one or more foreign languages. At one Ivy League college, the position governs 260,000 slides and oversees reference and circulation services. Salary range is $19,000 to $24,000.

A systems librarian plans, develops, and implements online catalogs; computer skills are essential. With experience, these positions pay $25,000 and up. A serials librarian works with periodicals, keeping track of hundreds of titles and supervising interlibrary loans, reference services, and instruction to library users. Reference librarians either staff or supervise the reference service, helping to plan and develop its programs. Familiarity with database searching is required, as are interpersonal skills and written and oral communication abilities. In university libraries, reference positions can command salaries as high as $45,000 at bigger facilities for senior staff. Public libraries offer jobs like children's librarian, requiring a background in social science and child-related subjects, and pay $20,000 and up. Catalogers classify English and foreign-language materials and need language and classification training. A young adult librarian needs outreach and organizational skills and can have extensive public contact with the target population, earning up to $25,000.

Outreach and extension libraries often serve rural or suburban communities; a driver's license is needed. Some facilities serve shut-ins or children, and strong communication skills are needed. Depending on the location, these jobs usually pay under $20,000 to start. At the coordinator level, requiring fund raising and public relations skills in addition to library experience, salaries range above $40,000 for a county-wide position.

At most institutions, a master's degree in library science is a one-year program; occasionally, it requires two years. Drexel University now offers a master's of science in information systems. Nowadays, academic libraries often request both an M.L.S. degree and a master's in a particular subject. Promotion opportunities are mainly into management positions. When her supervisor left, Kuhta was promoted to her present position as director of the main library in the Foundation Center's system. She is responsible for locating, hiring, and training the library staff, as well as scheduling, program planning, budgeting, new programs development, and coordinating with other departments. Kuhta reports to the president and has a staff of ten, who provide the library services described previously. She also serves as the liaison among all four Foundation Center operated libraries, making recommendations to the other libraries, answering questions from their staff members, and working with them on new programs. She visits each office once or twice a year, and their directors come to her office also, so that each center knows what the others are doing.

Kuhta has full hiring authority and recommends the budget for staffing; the president and three officers make decisions that set the caps on staffing. Kuhta appointed a senior librarian to be the library's assistant director, so she could participate on a task force for new income sources, which involved weekly meetings. The best part of the job, she finds, is planning. She enjoys finding new ways of doing things, establishing a team, putting together a good group, and working with them. "No one's in this just for themselves." She also likes the "group work, finding out what nonprofits need, the opportunity to learn, and endless reading."

Aside from the management path, another possible direction for librarians is the new field of information broker, a for-profit consultant who obtains the copyrights to many databases and charges a fee for providing information to business and professional clients.

COMMUNITY COORDINATOR AT A CANCER TREATMENT PROGRAM

Santa Monica's Wellness Community, says staff member Flo Porter, is helping to "change bigotry and bias, the prejudice towards cancer patients." Porter leads orientation sessions for new participants and interviews applicants for the 15 weekly groups of 12 members each. Recovered cancer patients lead the groups at the Wellness Community, where, according to Porter, the aim is "to motivate and encourage, showing participants that cancer is not a minority condition." Porter's own bout with cancer led to two major decisions: a divorce and a return to school part-time to complete a B.A. degree. Three years later, she had a degree in psychology and a strong desire to work with people.

Although her immediate job before joining the Wellness Community was a five-year stint at a bank, most of her previous experience pointed toward human service. In four years at a "classic settlement house," her work with mental hygiene clinics reflected an interest in psychology. "From ages 19 to 22, I was trained in home visits to help patients with budget problems. I loved working with people, and making a difference."

Her job now is in a cheerful, homelike building in a central Santa Monica location. It is intentionally inviting to patients, whose company Porter enjoys. "The weekly meetings are laugh-filled," she reports. "I like watching people flourish, bloom, and change." All of the services are free, and the facilities are new. The special events are fun, and, because it is located near Los Angeles, many celebrities visit the Wellness Community. Barbara Eden does their public service announcements, Jonathan Winters plays Santa Claus at their Christmas party, and when we visited, Jane Fonda was about to drop by to talk about helping them. Although Porter's official hours are 11 A.M. to 5 P.M., "I must attend the functions, so there are lots of evening hours. I love the events, although it's unpaid time. I enjoy meeting Jane Fonda, Tom Hayden, and other stars. Extra tasks are expected of you here."

The cooperative, team-oriented spirit is pervasive, and the hope is that all staff, eventually, will be recovered cancer patients. Porter believes, "you can't really understand the problems if you haven't had them. It helps to have faced your own death, and lived with the fear."

When Porter hires staff for the four-year-old program, she looks for "people who are compassionate, with high energy. It helps if they can contribute money. Our staff are mostly young, mostly female; the interns are graduate students. We give a lot of burn-out (prevention) work for staff, holding retreats. The job gets you over the fear of death." The current service providers include eight interns, seven therapists, two full-time staff, one half-time staff, and many volunteers.

The licensed therapists are paid $100 a week for each group. Interns see patients individually for six sessions. The Wellness Community calls its population "participants," not patients, and uses attitude as a healing tool, encouraging participants to control more of their own lives. A medical board verifies attitudinal changes in the participants, who usually become more cooperative, optimistic, and less angry at their doctors. Participants serve on the program's advisory board. The Wellness Community's board of directors, meeting every three months, includes businessmen who help with expansion plans and fund raising.

Porter obviously enjoys her work and is deeply committed to the organization. Are there any negatives? She immediately mentions "sadness at losing participants. The salary is low, with no fringes, no medical insurance, and no pension.

We get only a free parking spot. I'd earn more with a master's degree."

A new branch in Glendale is under consideration, and as the Wellness Community expands and matures, benefits to employees may evolve. With the costs of hospital care soaring, community-based and outpatient programs will multiply, so if you are drawn toward working with seriously ill individuals, opportunities exist. Some jobs may require (or prefer) a master's degree in social work, while others will accept undergraduate degrees in psychology, social work, and related areas. The most important traits for a job helping cancer patients, or others with life-threatening diseases, are empathy and commitment. You must be able to understand these people's complex emotional needs and feel deeply drawn to help. Often, dedicated workers are drawn to this type of service because of their own or a loved one's experience with the particular condition. The jobs can be in hospices, cancer care groups, medical centers, and community agencies. Salaries can vary widely, depending, in part, on the size of the organization and the degree requirements for the particular position.

ELEMENTARY AND SECONDARY EDUCATION

Physics Teacher at a Northeastern Private School

Englishman Tony Godwin observes that Trinity, the nation's longest consistently running independent school, is "older than the United States." Founded in 1709 by Queen Anne, the school was originally set up by Trinity Church as a free charity and has evolved into an outstanding private school with a growing endowment. The school's facilities are excellent, even including carpeted hallways. Naturally, the tuition supporting this is high: $8,000 a year does not include books or trips. Trinity has a dress code, prohibiting makeup and requiring jackets and slacks for the girls. Boys wear collared shirts and ties.

Godwin had started out as an engineer in England but lasted only one year. "I couldn't care about trimming one-millionth of an inch off a tin can," he reflects. "The high decibel level in the factory was harmful, and the office situation had lots of politics. I couldn't enjoy dealing with the union, either." Shifting to education proved a happier choice. "Teaching is one of the most rewarding jobs. I can't imagine anything nobler. You can't have as much fun in other fields...one of the reasons for the low pay. We get autonomy and no politics, or a very minimal amount."

Godwin teaches four classes a day, down from five last year. This leaves six class periods a day in which to see students. Trinity offers "phenomenal individual attention to kids. Students face terrific pressure to do well, from peers, parents, and some faculty. [They] get relentless daily homework." Godwin becomes well-acquainted with his 60 to 80 students each year. "I see the parents, too, at dinner, or skiing, or on summer house visits. It's fun. I get to know some of them very well. Alumni come back to say hello and take you to dinner."

Trinity's reputation for hard work and excellence attracts students from very wealthy families. Godwin unabashedly enjoys his exposure to "American affluence." He teaches math and physics to "extremely bright, well-motivated students, in classes averaging 15. I have almost no discipline problems. Academically, it's very high-flying, stimulating for both teachers and students." One hundred percent of the 800 pupils go on to college, mostly to Ivy League schools. Trinity has a faculty of 90, and "an army of maintenance and administrative staff. Communication is better and the people more neighborly than in an English school," Godwin finds.

Godwin, having decided after vacationing in America that he would like to live here, got his job by answering Trinity's ad in the overseas section of the British Times Education supplement, a weekly. The headmaster interviewed and hired him in London; Trinity handled all the legal aspects of his relocation. Godwin credits America's serious shortage of science teachers with his easy job hunt.

American private schools have long been known for good

working conditions and poor pay. Since his arrival nearly four years ago, Godwin reports an average salary increase of 12 to 14 percent each year. "Trustees have worked hard to raise faculty salaries; within two or three years, Trinity will pay more than the local board of education. With the tax advantages for private education, independent schools can pay more to get better staff." When the school split from Trinity Church, it kept the land but no money; Trinity School raised $3 million for an endowment, which is now an ongoing program. As the endowment grows, Trinity provides more scholarships. This is expected to take pressure off tuition fees to raise faculty salaries. Among the "flawless conditions at the school," Godwin cites a new theater, which brings professional acting troupes to mingle with the students.

In addition to his teaching responsibilities, Godwin coaches girls' varsity soccer and boys' junior varsity tennis. He finds coaching enough fun that "I'd do it if they didn't pay me"; however, he does receive a modest fee for each match and every practice session. However, he comments that "you don't do it for the money. It's nice to be connected to the students in other ways. It improves relationships with the kids, leading to better control." Godwin feels his athletic skills were a big help in his being hired, as well as his corporate experience. "Independent schools look not just for education credits, but a well-rounded person, in and out of school."

Godwin likes the hours and the vacations, which include 17 weeks off each year. In fact, though, he teaches a six-week summer program, in which students can do advanced physics work, three hours a day. "Otherwise," Godwin states, "I'd get bored." Hours are approximately 8:30 A.M. to 4 P.M. but vary. "We don't punch in," Godwin notes. The last class ends at 3:10 P.M., and he often goes jogging. College recommendations take up half his Christmas vacation. Each recommendation is individual, requiring several hours to prepare.

Among the "perks" he cites are free lunch all year, with superb food, in the school's cafeteria. Also, says Godwin, "benefits are excellent, comparable to any industry: full dental, major medical, a typical pension plan (vested at ten years). The tennis courts, weight room, and Nautilus machines are always available and free to faculty."

Another advantage for faculty is Trinity House, a below-market-rate residential tower around the corner, owned by the school. When he arrived in America, Godwin was shocked at the difficulty of finding affordable housing. Having hoped to spend about $300 a month in rent, to allow for ski trips, he waited a year and a half for a large studio in Trinity House, where 25 or 30 of his colleagues live. While he does not socialize with the faculty, Godwin often runs into Trinity students at clubs or discos.

Apart from enjoying the students, Godwin's recommendations for prospective teachers are as follows:

- Know your subject.
- It helps not to have physical defects—kids are merciless.
- Wit and humor will help you get attention.
- You need stamina. Keep fit; you'll get every virus for the first year or two.
- A relaxed demeanor is important. Kids make mistakes, so don't punish too readily.
- Stress is high, especially while you're learning to keep control. Discipline comes only after a few years.
- Be scrupulously fair—whether you like your students or not.
- If you have a funny name, change it.

Godwin also remarks that good managers do not succeed by authority, but by leadership. Poor teachers use authority, good teachers don't have to. Relaxing and being yourself in a classroom takes experience.

Godwin, who was head of a physics department before leaving England, wants to be a headmaster by his mid 40s. He likes running things and does not enjoy taking orders. "English, history, and religion teachers are in a good position at Trinity; the school was planned around them, and the city supports those interests. There's no science museum here!" Godwin plans to relocate eventually, to seek a school more oriented to the sciences.

He cites some other drawbacks to his profession as well. "Teaching leads to burnout at some phase. Enthusiasm will probably return after a sabbatical or a stint at administration. Teaching is always stressful. Unbelievable logic keeps the pay low. Education is always cut in budget crises." Speaking as a foreign observer, he thinks, "deregulation under Reagan will improve education here, although segmenting the field into those who can or can't afford it. Once you make the school a business, it seems to flourish. Supply and demand principles operate in a capitalistic society."

Turnover at Trinity averages only about 10 percent a year; staff in more senior positions stay longer, due to added responsibilities (such as the chairmanship of a department).

Listening to Godwin's enthusiasm and visiting the school, with its attractive layout and outstanding facilities, suggests that teaching is a golden opportunity. To obtain some perspective, we asked an inner city high school faculty member for the past 22 years to compare his experience to Godwin's private school portrait.

Guidance Counselor at a Public High School

Formerly a social studies teacher and coach, Len Mednick shifted to counseling four years ago, and cites its diversity as a key reward.

> I manage an office and coordinate four diverse programs which include low-ability kids needing remediation as well as average-ability students needing motivation. I disseminate scholarship information to our college-bound seniors (about 75 percent of the graduating class) and am the omnibus counselor to six classes, or 180 other students. I interact with college officials and parents of all shapes, sizes, ages, and colors. I'm experiencing an interesting phenomenon lately: high school kids stay the same age, but in my eyes their par-

ents get younger and younger! When I started teaching, there were some students older than I was. With a case load of 450 a year, I've had an opportunity to make lifelong friendships with people I'd never have come into contact with otherwise—successful corporate executives, comedians, dancers, doctors, actors, lawyers.

Like Tony Godwin, Mednick finds his work environment very stimulating.

> Faculty have so many avenues for involvement and input into the operations of the school. We create our own courses and programs. Organizations abound to absorb the creative energy in the buildings: seven publications and forty clubs. As a nontraditional school featuring learning modules and an eight-hour day, an automatic halo effect surrounds the faculty selected to work here. I think my colleagues are exceptional people, well-read in contemporary affairs, avid theatergoers and travelers.

Some of the other "perks" Mednick cites are conferences at museums, historic sites, or universities, and the opportunity to see at least one play a week at one-third the regular price and to go to advance screenings of new movies. Mednick also mentions the long summer vacations, which have allowed him to spend recent summers in Paris, the Greek Islands, and Africa.

Reflecting on his long career in education, Mednick comments:

> So many executives in corporate America seem to take pride in leaving the weekend free for their families. I always wonder what happened to their family dynamic during the rest of the week. I make a comfortable living ($45,000 a year), but more importantly, I have the time to *do* my living. I used to coach j. v. basketball for some extra money; now I'm faculty advisor to the tennis club. I get free court time and play with some excellent young players. The bottom line is I like the work. It's fun, it's challenging. There are adult problems and real growth to be seen. It's a constantly changing kalei-

doscope of faces and personalities; the job keeps me young, optimistic, and sensitive.

Whatever their specialty, counselors help people make decisions. They listen, support, encourage, and assist people with physical, emotional, educational, or vocational problems. With links to community agencies, they can refer clients to other services or resources that can help in specific ways. Counselors may use diagnostic or psychological instruments to collect data or make assessments. Keeping records of their findings and interactions with clients is another responsibility all counselors share. Apart from meeting with individuals, counselors may also work with groups, to discuss a problem common to all the members. This format works well with orientation or occupational information topics, for example. The counselor plans and facilitates the group session, striving to engage all the members in a discussion of shared concerns.

The largest specialty in the counseling profession is guidance, or counseling in schools. In the early 1980s, America's high schools alone employed 48,000 guidance counselors. All their responsibilities are geared to helping students fulfill their potential. Guidance counselors work with teachers to resolve a student's difficulties, communicate with parents, and collaborate with school administrators on behalf of students. They give information, conduct surveys and research, and plan programs. To promote growth and learning, guidance counselors take an interest in every aspect of the students and their lives. Frequent clients in high school guidance offices are the underachieving students, or the potential dropouts. Counseling services can make a measurable difference in attendance or dropout rates. At the high-school level, counselors can set up career days or college fairs to provide students with information related to their postgraduation plans. One of Len Mednick's colleagues, Janet Lipschultz, is their school's college adviser. She coordinates a city-wide college fair each autumn, at which some 300 higher-education institutions present their offerings to thousands of high school seniors. Lipschultz feels her job carries a great deal of autonomy. She regularly visits colleges to keep her knowledge of offerings and admissions policies current. Results of her work are visible every spring, when students gain admission to the nation's most prestigious colleges by following her advice. She tries to match students to appropriate schools, and reaps the satisfaction of seeing many of her recommendations met.

At the elementary school level, a smaller corps of counselors works to identify children's needs and assess their home backgrounds. They may conduct tests to evaluate potential. A large part of their work is pinpointing problems and possible causes. Counselors in grade schools have a one-to-one relationship with the kids and tend to work in a very short time frame.

College counselors try to facilitate success and promote maturity, by working in a broad spectrum of student-personnel areas. Some 3,000 colleges, both public and private, provide advisement in financial aid, student employment, admissions, job placement, mental health or crisis intervention, graduate school, housing, academic or course issues, and the special needs of foreign students.

Vocational counselors can work in public employment agencies, social service organizations, or universities. They help clients identify their interests, recommend appropriate training or education, and furnish leads or resources for job hunting. Working with adults, many of whom are contemplating a career change, vocational (or career) counselors map out a plan of steps for the client to follow. These experts teach job-hunting skills, including interviewing, resume writing, and application procedures.

Over 13,000 rehabilitation counselors help people adjust to and cope with disabilities or handicaps, which may be physical, emotional, mental, or social. Some disabilities will be temporary. Rehabilitation counseling, a growing field, offers jobs in schools, with handicapped or mentally retarded children. In adult rehabilitation, the counselors strive to build trust and confidence, and to help the client admit and accept a disability so that a rehabilitation program can be planned. The counselor and client set goals for the future together. The counselor may help locate jobs, meet with families and training agencies for the client, and serve as a liaison to the rest of the community. Rehab counselors often give tests to evaluate clients' abilities. Specialties within rehabilitation include drugs, alcoholism, blindness, and other handicaps. Many rehabilitation agencies are state or federally funded; they frequently provide training, placement, and follow-up services to clients. Some of the positions require a civil service test. All rehabilitation counselors work to develop the individual's self-esteem and independent functioning, and to formulate occupational plans, given the client's limitations.

A master's degree, while not always required, is a strong advantage for counseling positions, and will become more esential as the field expands. Three new specialties are emerging today: geriatric counseling, pastoral counseling, and marriage or family counseling. With the over 65 population growing steadily, the need for skilled, sensitive counselors trained in aging and adult psychology will expand steadily. Ministers, priests, rabbis, and other members of the clergy have always offered guidance as part of their services to congregants. Recently, members of religious organizations have begun to seek professional training in graduate counseling programs, some of which offer special courses in pastoral counseling. With America's high divorce rate and rise in single-parent families, the need for marriage and family counseling is evident. Graduate training is now available, and counselors can work for social service agencies, mental health clinics, or in private practice. Master's programs in counseling are widely available, requiring 36 to 60 credits of course work, depending on the college and the specialty.

Being a successful counselor requires that you like people and can take a sincere interest in your clients. Interviewing skills and listening abilities are key traits. Empathy, or sensitivity to the other person's feelings and perspective, is another essential. Counselors also need flexibility, consistency, a sense of humor, negotiating ability, a talent for problem solving, and rapport with many different types of people.

The academic schedule is one of the primary advantages of teaching; most teachers enjoy the early hours and generous vacations. While many educators travel or study during their time off, others are involved in second careers, for additional income or variety or both. Len Mednick's colleagues are typical of the profession. A music teacher plays piano on weekends at an elegant waterfront restaurant; an English instructor sells residential real estate. Another coworker owns an ice cream parlor a few miles from the high school, where students have part-time jobs and their classmates come to buy. Capitalizing on strong interpersonal skills and persuasive abilities, teachers everywhere are frequently attracted to sales fields. Travel, real estate, and direct sales (like Avon products or Tupperware) are popular. We know a junior high school teacher who runs a pottery studio and shop on afternoons and weekends.

For another viewpoint on careers in education, we went to a different type of teacher, a highly trained woman who has recently left the field.

Special Education Teacher at a Parochial School

"Special ed means you're more involved with the child and family. Classes are smaller than usual, with a maximum of ten students. If you enjoy giving to others, special ed is *it*," say Sue Woodner (her name has been changed at her request), who taught deaf, emotionally disturbed, and physically handicapped preschoolers for 13 years. She has an M.A. in audiology and a B.A. in speech and hearing pathology. The joy of her work, she found, was in "molding human beings." Many of her deaf students had hearing parents who were unable to cope with them. "When they got to me, the kids didn't talk or use sign language; teaching language or communication skills was incredible. The parents couldn't handle them at home, so most of the children's social behaviors were unacceptable. The parents either didn't know how to communicate, or felt so guilty at having a deaf child that they gave the kid the run of the house."

Woodner also enjoyed counseling students and working with the families, in cooperation with the school psychologist. She found that

> you make a real impact on another human being by your efforts, and see a change. You must structure the day so they can learn, building different approaches because not every person learns the same way. I found lots of warmth from working with kids. These people shouldn't be considered wasted human beings; they can live a fairly normal life if you've given them some skills and self-respect. It's creative and fun for the teacher.

On working at a Catholic school for the deaf, she observes:

> My kids went from open classrooms with me to a nun who had every five minutes scheduled. They did fine in both settings. I couldn't have handled a school where kids were compelled to go to religious training every day. Special ed kids can't go to regular services, though, so this is the only place they can get religious training. Faculty included many non-Catholics, and the school was open to religious differences. The majority of teachers in Catholic schools today are lay.

The school where she worked was largely funded by state money. Woodner believes opportunities are good for jobs in special education as "federal and state laws now require local school districts to provide education for handicapped children within commuting distance." Salaries follow the usual teaching pattern, increasing with seniority in the public school system and being generally lower in parochial or private schools. When she left her job two years ago, Woodner was earning about $25,000. After two years in the personnel department of a corporate real estate firm, she has discovered, "business is more selfish," and is considering returning to her educational career. She switched fields because her coworkers had become very unstimulating and she found no source of creativity at the school anymore. She had never stopped enjoying the direct work with the children, however, and misses it in her new role.

In career-change workshops, discontented teachers complain about either low pay or the frustration of having to provide as much discipline as education. Many cited the low prestige in which the public holds their profession as discouraging. Interestingly, though, when they explore other possibilities, teachers in our workshops often conclude that it would take too long to reach their current salary level in another field, or that it really would not be worth sacrificing the convenient hours and generous vacations to start over again in a new occupation.

Teachers get jobs by applying to the local board of education, which will place educators in schools with openings. Aspiring faculty members can get jobs by applying directly to a school where they would like to work, being hired by the principal in a primary school, or after interviewing with the department chairperson in a secondary school, who makes a recommendation to the principal. State certification, attained after completing particular state-approved courses, is always required. Check the requirements in your own state to see which courses are needed. When there is a teacher shortage, arrangements are made by local boards of education for emergency certification. Each state grants certification after reviewing the credentials of an applicant.

A license is not required by all school systems but is provided by the local board where necessary. It is attained after completing certain state-approved courses for certification, and then passing an exam. Check with the board in the community where you would like to teach to find out if a license is needed. A new trend toward a national teaching exam is beginning to gain momentum. It would allow successful candidates to teach in all states (provided they met the specific course requirements, if any, for a license in a particular place).

HEALTH SERVICE
Nursing Supervisor, Urban Medical Center

Chuck Srock had wanted to be a physician and elected to major in nursing instead of premed, to get the strong science background he would need. Having really enjoyed the R.N. program, he felt the rewards of a doctor's career were not worth four more years of school, and entered the job market at age 21. "Nurses can get jobs anywhere; you pretty much write your own ticket," Srock reports. "Most R.N.s have a need to be needed—often extreme." Originally an intensive-care-unit (I.C.U.) nurse, he moved to open heart surgery and was recruited, after 11 years, from Philadelphia to the Los Angeles area.

The hierarchy of nursing positions, from bottom to top, is as follows:

- Nurse's aide
- L.P.N. (Licensed Practical, or Vocational, Nurse)
- Staff R.N. (on a unit)
- Charge nurse (running a shift)
- Head nurse (running a whole floor)
- Supervisor (of all units on a shift; usually held by the assistant director of nurses)
- Director of nurses

According to Srock, his promotion to nursing supervisor means, "I'm the resource person for the hospital. I have to know policy and procedures, and may occasionally bend the rules. Good public relations skills are necessary, to keep patients, staff, administration, and doctors happy. It's a juggling act. Supervisors have to have the best nursing skills and the clinical background to evaluate I.C.U. nurses. You'll be both troubleshooter and backup person." Srock works three 12-hour shifts a week, from 7 P.M. to 7 A.M., when he is the highest official on duty. His medium-sized hospital has 140 beds, several ambulatory units, and good equipment. His job no longer involves patient care, so Srock does part-time I.C.U. work, free-lance, on days off in order to keep his skills up. He often volunteers extra hours at his own hospital, or works at other hospitals to see what is new in the field. He chose not to be on salary, electing to be paid as an hourly employee with a supervisor title, and works about 60 hours a week. While employees get 12 sick days a year, managers are expected to be there. "It's hard to get replacements for a supervisor. You're not expected to take 12 days; three is the standard." Nurses in many locations get "comp time," but nurses in California hospitals no longer receive this.

Srock found some striking differences in nursing on the West Coast after his Pennsylvania experience. I.C.U. and ambulatory nurses are paid $17,000 to $20,000 in the East, compared with $20,000 to $35,000 in California, for example. On this discrepancy in pay, he remarks,

> We had three nurses for ten patients in Philadelphia, for $6.25 an hour in 1980. California state law required a maximum of two patients per nurse in intensive care. The starting rate is $15 an hour. In open-heart cases, the ratio is one to one. California has 12-hour shifts, with time-and-a-half rates for the last four hours, so you could work two full-time jobs for $70,000. The East Coast simply pays lower.

As for benefits, Srock finds, "nurses are stronger out West, because of the union. Patient loads are heavier in the East, costs higher in the West."

What is it like for a man in a profession traditionally dominated by women? Srock feels "the entry of men into nursing has led to higher salaries. Male managers are more direct and less catty. Women are less confronting." Being male has been both a help and a hindrance to Srock.

> With more men in nursing today, women managers were threatened. The hospital administrators liked men because they didn't take maternity leave. Wives come and go in nursing, depending on their husband's income. Male R.N.s concentrate on key areas: operating room, emergency room,

intensive care unit, or psychiatry. I've never had strange reactions from patients.

Nowadays his rewards are primarily monetary, but he reminisces on past days when

> patients were more appreciative; now they act like they're at the Hilton. You learn the ideals in nursing school, providing a therapeutic community. Reality shock is finding tender loving care doesn't work with street-gang patients who have chest wounds. Patients used to send cards, flowers, or candy when they got home. It's rare if that happens now, although occasionally you get a special patient.

The negatives of the field, Srock says, are "long hours, and strange hours." Nurses are expected to work on holidays, for instance. Although he insists on New Year's Eve off, he has worked every Christmas. He also notes that rising health costs have lead to unappreciative patients. "Since hospitals vie for customers now, patients complain to administrators."

Srock is highly sensitive to the shifting shortages in his profession, and points out that

> the need for I.C.U. nurses is growing, because of the high burnout rate. The average nurse stays three to four years, works closely with M.D.s, and can get a lot of respect. Aggressive, go-getting types do well in I.C.U.; for example, if a physician is wrong, the I.C.U. nurse will tell him. Hospitals are often so short staffed in I.C.U., they'll train you and provide a salary during training. I was trained eight hours a day for eight days at one hospital. I.C.U. is very intense and can lead to management, emergency room, or clinical work.

Because I.C.U. nursing requires management skills and assertiveness, a majority of supervisors have this sort of experience. In Srock's nursing class of 20, only three entered I.C.U. as a specialty. They got paid more because of the shortage and the difficulty of the assignment.

Another growth area is ambulatory, or urgent, care, a 24-hour miniemergency clinic. Dual benefits of this trend are lower costs for the patient and good management training for nurses.

Sometimes opportunities in health-care fields depend on the number of physicians in the field. Nurse-anesthetist was a promising area for some time, Srock recalls, but at present there is a surplus of M.D.s. Nurse-practitioners can have their own office and can treat minor maladies and give allergy shots—much like the old-time general physicians. Srock believes that nurse-anesthetists could provide cheaper patient care and free up M.D. specialists. Unfortunately, however, "the powerful American Medical Association squashed the idea. In California, Kaiser will train the nurse-practitioners, who can write prescriptions in two states. Opportunities are best where M.D.s are in short supply." (Kaiser-Permanente Health Clinics, based in California, is one of the earliest health maintenance organizations established in America.)

A new problem facing the nursing profession is the issue of lawsuits, which are increasing in the health-care field. While a hospital's insurance covers its staff, a nurse working as an independent contractor may feel compelled to purchase individual insurance. Srock cautions against this. "Having malpractice coverage personally can make you the target of a lawsuit. It might help you get named in the suit."

Marla Goodman, a nurse recruiter based in southern California, takes a different view. "An an individual contractor," she advises, "you need your own malpractice insurance, which an institution probably covers for full-time employees." Goodman works for a nurse's registry, which acts as a per-diem placement agency for R.N.s. Insurance requirements may vary among registries. Rates of pay vary within the hospitals themselves, Goodman explains. "A unit pays better than a general floor nurse position." California has the highest nursing pay scale, but opportunities for beginners are limited.

> All California hospitals require one year of on-staff experience. The only opportunity for a new R.N. (with a B.S. degree) is in nursing homes, or working through small central registries. Through student training at a hospital, you might be able to line up a future job, once they've gotten to

know you and like your work. A hospital has to spend extra time to train a new nurse.

Goodman's registry requires nurses to be registered (which means licensed), and to have an annual physical and tine test for tuberculosis. They also need a cardiopulmonary resuscitation card, available from the American Heart Association, the Red Cross, or in-service training at many hospitals.

In recent years, the demand for nurses in America appears to have escalated dramatically, with constant openings occurring. In fact, Goodman claims,

> the shortage is in spurts. Burnout is common, largely because R.N.s are not fulfilled just doing nursing. To postpone burnout, divert your interests within the field. You can become a visiting nurse, working through the public health service, or do home care, which requires affiliating with a for-profit placement agency. Home care currently pays $14 to $17.50 an hour. You might also become a nurse-practitioner and work through a central registry. The registries are competitive; some give health insurance and vacation benefits to attract the best employees.

The most common complaints Goodman hears from nurses concern the need to work unorthodox shift schedules or the unvarying nature of patient care. The patient/nurse ratio is set by state law, so it can differ from place to place. Goodman notes some complaints about assignments in nursing homes, where standards for patient care or cleanliness may be a bit lax.

Apparently, however, exceptions do exist. Professor Ellen Glascock, former chairwoman of the Allied Health Department at St. Francis College, described two "fabulous" nursing homes run by nuns:

> At the Carmelites' home, the level of care is high. A cocktail hour for patients and guests is held daily. The facility is run by the nuns, with some lay staff. The Little Sisters of the Poor, an order supported by begging, provide residential care and have very skilled nurses. Their "independent living" option provides apartments nearby, with separate kitchens

and care immediately available. They've created a "mini-mall" with a coffee shop, mailbox, little store, and park bench. The staff at both sites love their work, and communicate the joy of service to everyone working there.

A recent development in patient care is the hospice, a residence for terminally ill patients where clinical features are minimized. Glascock observes a very high sense of satisfaction among hospice staff, most of whom have a high service motive and are deeply idealistic. "It's a chance to really make a difference," says Glascock. "They provide a lot of employee support. Apart from the terminally ill patients, it's not like a hospital. One suburban hospice had cathedral ceilings, carpeting, and patios the patient could get to easily."

"A good nurse," Glascock reports, "is motherly, tireless, glad to help a dying patient. Thick skin is required, as you'll be ordered around. Intellectual drive is not a plus." According to Glascock, the key questions to ask yourself if you are considering a nursing career are:

- Are you dedicated to doing the job?
- Do you realize the psychic and physical toll it will exact?
- Can you accept low rewards and little acknowledgment?
- Would you prefer being an Indian to being a chief (or, at most, a very limited chief)?

Glascock, too, thinks the employment outlook is good. She finds that there always seem to be jobs available for nurses and health technicians, and that the good ones move up. She remarked that her students become nurses

> for convenience, security, and proximity to home and family. The field meshed well with having children. Most nurses don't look beyond nursing and aren't very interested in moving up. One of my former students, a male, now sells pacemakers. It's hard to leap from nursing to the administration side, although some hospitals now call the director of nursing a vice president.

A good advancement move, Glascock feels, is to the nurse-practitioner level. She has noticed that "male nurses rise rapidly, as soon as they graduate. Most are in supervisory positions four years after a degree."

Of 225 allied health majors at St. Francis, many are already nurses, returning to school to pursue a B.S. degree, which is a virtual requirement for moving up. However, the degree provides no training in the management skills a head nurse needs. Glascock notes that long-time nurses occasionally have to go back to a B.S. in nursing program.

> One of my students actually had to work on the floor she used to run, in order to get her B.S.N. The nursing profession is hurting itself by taking a narrow view. I advise taking another graduate degree, like an M.B.A., for career advancement. In the typical feminine stereotype, nurses avoid math and statistics courses, [but] they have to read budgets as head nurses; to work as an independent practitioner, you need business skills. Don't get an M.A. in nursing—it's just more of the same.

Most of Glascock's students earn over $25,000. They have extensive experience but complain about the lack of autonomy, patients dying, and terrible working conditions, including noise, no place to sit, and the lack of privacy. Adequate supplies or equipment are sometimes lacking, too, as is acknowledgment from supervisors. Like Marla Goodman, Glascock cites frequent burnout. "They have all the typical women-in-management problems," reports the instructor of a course by that name.

Just as nursing has become more specialized, the health fields in general have diversified and created expanding opportunities in new areas. At St. Francis, the Allied Health Department includes respiration therapists, and lab technicians, who are trying to move up in their fields to become department heads or associate directors. Many of these students, according to Glascock, are minority members, climbing up the socioeconomic ladder. Almost half of them are men, and they take a longer view than do most nurses, planning ahead to become department managers or start a related business, such as home care or a private lab. Glascock says that the respiration therapy specialty is now being upgraded to a more professional status. "Previously, the field had a licensed practical nurse-type training, and those long-time workers are now the department heads, insecure with new graduates."

The health-service fields reflect changes in societal needs. Demographic shifts have led to expanded geriatric services and the development of the hospice concept, two good areas for employment. New laws that benefit the handicapped and the elderly mean more jobs in those specialties. Rising health-care costs, trumpeted by legislators and the media, mean more training programs for paraprofessionals, who cost less than their more expensively, extensively educated colleagues.

The range of therapeutic areas within health care continues to multiply. What these areas have in common is that each treats a specific disability and improves the patients' quality of life. Here are some very brief descriptions of most of the therapeutic specialties; Appendix B gives suggestions on where to get further information.

Respiration (or Inhalation) Therapist

These professionals treat people with cardiorespiratory problems. They can provide temporary relief for asthma or emphysema sufferers, or emergency care for stroke, heart attack, shock, drowning, head injuries, or poisoning. They assist patients after surgery as well. Respiration therapists use special equipment and may train patients to employ these devices. Ninety percent of the jobs are in hospitals, entailing shift work and a great deal of standing.

One reason inhalation therapists have to spring into action quickly is that a patient will die if oxygen is cut off for more than five minutes. They deliver immediate care in all age groups, from newborn infants to the very elderly. Respiration therapists give medications, show patients breathing exercises to keep their lungs clear, and apply suction to remove obstructions to breathing.

Respiration therapists work in hospitals, clinics, or nursing homes, most often in the emergency room, nursery, medical-surgical department, or intensive care unit. Home-care services are now beginning to offer respiration therapy as part of their treatments to clients, creating a new employment possibility for practitioners.

In the early 1980s, America had some 46,000 employed respiration therapists. They are trained in hospitals, medical schools, colleges, or vocational schools; most programs lead to an associate in arts (A.A.) degree. Of the 200 training programs approved by the Committee on Allied Health Education, only 20 confer the B.A. in this field. Course work includes anatomy, physics, chemistry, physiology, microbiology, math, and technical training.

Respiration therapists must be detail-oriented team workers with mechanical ability and manual dexterity. They should enjoy working with people and be sensitive to the physical and psychological needs of their patients. Population growth combined with new diagnostic and treatment procedures have created many new jobs in this area. American demographics are changing; an aging population will have more frequent heart and lung problems, and will require more surgery for other reasons. Advancement possibilities are to the position of director of a respiration department or into other management roles; experienced inhalation therapists can become educators in the specialty. Starting salaries are generally in the teens; larger hospitals offer the best rates.

Physician's Assistant

Unlike most doctors, the physician's assistant (P.A.) is perceived as very approachable. They often handle patient relationships and answer all sorts of questions. Because they inspire less awe than physicians, patients will talk readily to a P.A. It is a growing specialty, and the physician's assistant can find jobs in health maintenance organizations (HMOs), hospitals, clinics, student health centers, and Emergency Rooms.

This occupation began in the 1960s, during an M.D. shortage; about 45 percent of physician's assistants work in sparsely populated areas underserved by M.D.s. The field grew rapidly in the 1970s, and hospitals and clinics today employ a growing number of P.A.s.

They are not doctors, yet they do treat patients. P.A.s perform many routine tests, explaining the procedure and their findings to patients. They can sew simple wounds, apply or remove splints or casts, give injections and immunizations, write prescriptions, and provide life-support measures (such as an intravenous hookup). They make referrals for further treatment and enter patient data on records. The P.A. frequently takes medical histories, and does followup phone calls to check on patients' progress. Working in an office, the P.A. treats minor injuries and makes tentative diagnoses. Often, they perform hospital rounds. Invariably, a P.A. works under the direction of a licensed supervising physician.

The work can be very fast paced. In a hospital outpatient clinic, a physician's assistant may see 15 or 20 patients a day, examine them thoroughly, and treat a wide range of complaints—from obesity to back injuries to simple sore throats. In addition, half a dozen emergency cases may arrive unexpectedly. Now that the field is maturing, P.A.s can specialize in a medical area, and work with an M.D. in orthopedics, pediatrics, urology, or surgery.

A majority of physician assistant jobs are in hospitals and clinics, and admission to training programs is becoming more competitive. Currently, about 60 accredited training programs are in operation. Related experience is an advantage in gaining admission. Your state may require you to pass a certification exam before practicing as a physician's assistant. This is a young field which grew rapidly at first, and fluctuates with the supply of physicians in the United States. Because many of the first P.A.s were Vietnam veterans with some military medical training, the occupation was heavily male dominated. It is now more open to women, and offers diverse responsibilities and challenges to both genders.

The job outlook is fair, because doctors are now abundant, and also because third-party reimbursement is usually not permitted for P.A. intervention. Opportunities may stem from expansion of health maintenance organizations and the aging American population.

Physician's assistants complete an approved training program, approximately two years long. Most applicants already have a B.A. and study anatomy, physiology, pharmacology, and microbiology, as well as taking supervised clinical courses. Thirty-five states require P.A.s to be certified by the National Committee on Certification of Physician's Assistants, Inc. Ongoing study is part of the field, to keep up with new medical developments. P.A.s should show leadership ability, confidence, stability, patience, a pleasant personality, and strong interpersonal skills. They have to explain things to patients, keep irregular hours, and deal with pressure. A key skill is being able to provide reassurance to the patients, and establish rapport quickly. Starting salaries for P.A.s are above $20,000, ranging near $40,000 with experience. The Veterans' Administration, for example, hires P.A.s for its hospitals at $19,000 to $31,000.

Occupational Therapist

As part of a team, occupational therapists (O.T.s) prepare patients to return to work, help restore their basic functions, and aid them in adjusting to their disabilities. Through various activities, often involving equipment, occupational therapists help mentally and physically disabled patients learn essential skills. Different problems require different approaches: toys and games with children, woodwork or leathercraft to develop motor coordination, plants and gardening for motivation and social skills.

Occupational therapists are on their feet a lot, putting in a 40-hour week that may include evenings or weekends. They have to work well with people of all ages and have a warm, friendly temperament that breeds trust and respect. Ingenuity is needed to adapt activities for individuals; skills, patience, and teaching ability are helpful.

A bachelor's degree in occupational therapy is required. Twenty-one states and the District of Columbia also require a license. Occupational therapists can be certified, earning the title of Registered Occupational Therapist. Aspiring O.T.s with a B.A. in some other field can get a master's degree in occupational therapy to enter the specialty. Course work includes biological, physical, and behavioral sciences. The job outlook is good, with salaries starting around $20,000 (higher in large metropolitan areas), and going to the mid $30,000s with some experience. America had 25,000 O.T.s in 1982, working mostly in hospitals, particularly in the rehabilitation and psychiatric units.

Dietitian

Of the 44,000 registered dietitians in 1982, more than half worked in health-care facilities, another 10 percent in child-care or residential-care facilities, and 10 percent in colleges, schools, and universities. Dietitians need organizational and administrative abilities, scientific aptitude, and good interpersonal skills. For a bachelor's degree, they study home economics, business administration, biology, health, math, and chemistry.

A *clinical dietitian* assesses nutritional needs, develops and implements care plans, and then evaluates and reports results. *Administrative dietitians* do large-scale planning and preparation in hospitals, prisons, schools, or other institutions. They supervise the planning, preparation, and serving of meals; set the budgets for and purchase food, equipment, and supplies; and prepare records and reports. They may also work with a *community nutrition* program, often part of a community health program, such as Meals On Wheels.

Nutrition is a field that changes rapidly, so it is important to keep up-to-date. Solid education in biochemistry is the best foundation. Basically, dietitians help people select food for nourishment, both in health and disease. Their efforts may improve the quality of life or prevent illness. Americans' growing interest in nutrition, health, and fitness has led to a new demand for nutritional information on food packages. It will also cause better job opportunities for trained dietitians.

A *research dietitian* needs a master of science degree, and works either independently or as part of a professional team, at a hospital, university, or public health agency. The work may focus mainly on the prevention of health problems. Some new specialties arising in the nutrition field, which may require an M.S. degree as well as some experience, are in pediatrics, critical care, renal (kidney) conditions, and diabetes. Sports nutrition is another evolving area, one in which dietitians provide information on weight control, vitamin or mineral supplements, and precompetition meals. Sports nutritionists mostly serve as consultants to teams or to individual athletes.

Dietitians, particularly in community nutrition, serve as health educators and diet counselors. They may work with families, pregnant women, or cardiovascular patients, and can treat obesity, alcoholism, and smoking.

Writing skills are becoming an increasing asset in the nutrition field. With more public interest, dietitians prepare materials and provide printed information. Some get involved in public relations or consumer information for manufacturers of packaged foods.

Salaries in nutrition vary greatly. For up-to-date information, check employment ads in the current issue of the *American Dietetic Association Journal*.

The professional credential, registered dietitian, is conferred by the American Dietary Association after completion of an approved dietitian internship, which may be coordinated as part of undergraduate or graduate training. An advanced degree is available, but not required for beginning jobs, which typically pay around $20,000, going to the mid $40,000s with experience. Opportunities in the field are good, due to expanding needs at hospitals and long-term health care facilities. (Note: Dietitians may work weekends, if they are part of a hospital staff.) Part-time work is sometimes available. Population growth, shifting demographics, increased attention to health and life-style, and the community health movement have all spurred the need for dietitians.

Physical Therapist

The therapy these professionals provide can be in the form of exercise, electrical stimulation, instruction, or massage, and requires knowledge of anatomy, physiology, human growth, and disease. Physical therapists (P.T.s) plan and administer treatment to restore bodily functions, relieve pain, and prevent or limit permanent disability for those with an injury or disease. Patients are accident victims, handicapped children, stroke victims, or others who may be suffering emotionally and physically, necessitating sensitivity and technical know-how. Treatment can be long, and the therapist/patient relationship may be important in attaining good results.

Physical therapists both train and treat their patients, aiming to relieve pain, restore functions, and prevent an injury from becoming a disability. Patients are referred by a physician; the physical therapist will often have to deal with the patient's anger, and must help the patient move past it to a useful treatment phase. This requires the P.T. to exercise great tact, and be gratified by very small results in a patient's progress.

A four-year degree is required for jobs today; by 1990, a graduate degree will be needed. Over 40,000 physical therapists are in practice already, and demand is far exceeding the supply. Great growth opportunity is reflected in jobs at nursing homes, hospitals, clinics, and research departments or pharmaceutical firms. A large East Coast voluntary teaching hospital recently advertised for a newly-graduated, state-registered physical therapist, offering $1,000 towards tuition reimbursement in addition to a salary of $26,500 to over $30,000.

Demand is multiplying as more and more doctors recognize the need for physical therapy. An aging population is more prone to injury, and the physical fitness movement has more Americans taking part in sports activities that produce injuries to some participants. New legislation requires physical therapy for certain handicapped groups, and more insurance coverage is becoming available for physical therapy treatment.

A particular growth area is sports medicine. The physical therapist will see an athlete after an injury, and plan and provide a treatment program to relieve pain, get the player back into action, and keep the person from further harm. Sports medicine employs many techniques, including massage, ultrasound, whirlpools, and hot packs. It requires strong interpersonal skills.

Every physical therapist designs exercise programs involving various types of equipment, ranging from weights and pulleys to floor mats, walkers, and parallel bars. They teach the patient and his or her family to use and care for wheelchairs, crutches, braces, or artificial limbs. Being creative in planning activities is part of the job's challenge. For example, one physical therapist organized a basketball game for postsurgery patients, who developed their arm muscles by playing from tilt-tables they had been strapped to.

Therapists evaluate the patient's condition and work with a physician to develop a treatment plan. They interact with patients' families, too. P.T.s can specialize in pediatrics, geriatrics, orthopedics, sports medicine, neurology, or cardiopulmonary problems. They may work evenings and weekends to accommodate patients. The tasks involved can be physically tiring, so stamina is important, as are patience, tact, resourcefulness, emotional stability, and manual dexterity.

About two-thirds of the jobs are in hospitals, the remainder in schools or residences for handicapped children, rehabilitation centers, or outpatient clinics. Physical therapists often become self-employed after they acquire adequate experience. All states require a license and at least a B.S. degree, which can lead to certification. A master's degree is available, too. The job outlook is excellent, due to anticipated growth in rehabilitation services, more programs to aid the disabled, higher incidence of birth defects, and an aging population. Salaries begin at $20,000 or more, advancing to the high $30,000s with some experience.

If you are interested in any of the health-service fields, try out the specialty by volunteering before you begin any training program. Make sure you like the work environment. Do you have the physical and emotional stamina to deal each day with patients' needs? Will the rewards (a patient's smile; someone relearning to walk) be enough to replenish you for your efforts the next day? Do not enter a health specialty without testing your tempermental suitability in a real-life setting.

COORDINATOR OF EMPLOYEE BENEFITS PROGRAM OF A LARGE MUNICIPAL HOSPITAL

Fred Hart (not his real name) has a Ph. D. in counseling psychology and works for an expanding hospital that already has over 10,000 employees. Six thousand of them are currently eligible for the employee health services provided by Hart's department, and he expects the other 4,000 to be eligible soon. In his newly created position, treating chemical dependencies, Hart reports to the medical director of employee services. Hart helps doctors recognize symptoms of drug withdrawal, trains supervisors to deal with drug or alcohol problems, which are often reflected in absenteeism, and provides clinical services, evaluations, and recommendations for change.

He will also teach a course on addiction in the Department of Psychiatry and has been invited to join a prestigious state committee dealing with the problem. His hours are 8:30 A.M. to 4:30 P.M. and are flexible.

Hart started out as a teacher, to avoid being drafted during the Vietnam War. He shifted to drug counseling before entering graduate school, and was hired by a multinational financial services firm as a counselor in their employee assistance program. He was promoted to a management post

The Program Department: Providing the Service 101

upon completing his doctorate. Though he was eager to return to a human services environment after five years in the business sector, Hart nevertheless finds his corporate background valuable.

> As the hospital moves toward a business mode, my experience with cost containment provides a useful sensitivity. Usually, good treatment equals good business sense. For example, we can set a lifetime limit of two hospitalizations for chemical dependency. We give the responsibility to the individual, forcing him or her to face reality. We help employees return to the work place.

Hart believes in fairly short-term intervention. His approach to work-place counseling emphasizes evaluation and diagnosis, leading to a referral. "We monitor the ongoing treatment. I could refer workers to the hospital's own psychiatry department, but they may not know enough about chemical dependency." For example, one of his patients was a male nurse with a 13-year Valium-amphetamine coaddiction. Hart sent him to a four-week residential facility, outside the hospital. Medical insurance paid for the employee's treatment.

A big difference from his banking days is that the financial services corporation for which he worked had no unions. The hospital has several, for different types of employees. While different benefits and contract provisions apply to each union, Hart finds that overall, "the product at the hospital is health care. Anyone I talk to here understands good treatment is the essential issue."

Hart managed to negotiate for the same salary he had been earning at the bank, and he finds the hospital's benefits package superior to his previous employer's. As for his work environment, he comments, "the hospital is less plush."

Counseling positions are available to people with master's degrees, and sometimes even bachelor's degrees in a related area. As Hart's experience shows, drug-addiction treatment programs are often an entry path into the field, and such programs frequently do not require a graduate degree. Salaries are slightly lower without a master's degree, of course, beginning in the mid teens for just a B.A. Alcohol treatment programs usually hire only recovered alcoholics for counseling positions.

Counseling differs from psychotherapy in that it is goal-oriented, tends to focus on a specific problem, and is generally short-term. Psychotherapy takes a gradual, less structured approach, dealing with the individual's entire personality and history, rather than concentrating on a single or immediate need. The two modalities use both one-to-one and group therapy. An important distinction is that many states do not cover counselors for third-party (insurance) payments, making a private practice difficult to build.

Hart's specialty, employee assistance, is a growth area in the corporate sector, attracting experienced counselors, social workers, and psychologists. In the nonprofit community, employee assistance programs are available at only the largest agencies, usually hospitals. (This is because of budgetary constraints, rather than disinterest in employees on the part of the not-for-profit agency.)

Many profit-making companies contract with a not-for-profit in their geographic area, so that trained professionals are available to help corporate employees with problems, at the company's expense. Occasionally, nonprofits provide out-placement or employee assessment services to corporations, for a fee.

PROFESSOR AT A SMALL METROPOLITAN COLLEGE

Associate Professor Ellen Glascock, who finished her Ph.D. in public health administration in 1981, has been at St. Francis College for nearly nine years. She is one of two women with tenure, out of a faculty of 68. "Tenure is both a blessing and a curse," she has discovered. "You get more security, but it's harder to leave. I do feel freer to express unpopular opinions—which I do almost all the time."

Glascock got her job by answering an ad in the local newspaper, and was originally hired as an assistant professor and department chairperson in allied health. St. Francis had been a private religious school until it switched to an independent liberal arts classification, to be eligible for more types of government funding. All students are still required to take nine credits of philosophy and three of religion. Faculty are divided along lay versus religious lines. "The old guard lay faculty are more like the [Franciscan] brothers, and are, in fact, more Catholic, parochial, and backward," Glascock says. Faculty members tend to be long-term, and Glascock found initially that she was "clearly 15 to 20 years younger" than her colleagues. "I was the only person who didn't smoke cigars." She was one of six women on the faculty at first; now there are 11.

Her relationship with St. Francis has a love/hate dimension. "I'm very comfortable, understand my students and their needs, and enjoy teaching the courses." She chose to give up the chairperson role after seven years, because it demanded "an extra 20 hours of work each week, for a differential of only $1,250 per term." She also found that the extra responsibilities affected her effectiveness as a teacher. Without those burdens, "I no longer feel I have a knot in my throat. On weekends now, I don't have to do anything. There's no constant crisis to respond to." Glascock is appreciating the fun of her work again, and "feeling like a new person. I've revised two of my four courses and am putting together two new courses, including an honors seminar, 'The Feminist View of the Core Curriculum.'"

She is on campus Mondays, Wednesdays, and Fridays, for a total of 36 hours a week, and spends up to five to ten additional hours working at home. "I'm quite adequately paid for a three-day week," she says. Vacations are generous: one month in winter, ten days at Easter, and late May through Labor Day. Glascock has calculated that she teaches three days a week, 30 weeks a year, for a maximum of 90 days a year. Her base salary is $30,000, for teaching four courses each term, which may include two sections of the same subject. "I'm not reinventing the wheel each term either," she points out. For one week each summer, she also conducts an intensive course at a large municipal hospital. This term, she is teaching six courses because, "without extra preparation, you get paid as an adjunct for those additional classes."

Now a member of the promotions and tenure committee, Glascock thinks the school has been too lenient about publishing. "It's not at all publish-or-perish here, but for a promotion, you must do some scholarly work, loosely classified. Book reviews count. I give a talk at the American Public Health Association each year, and an abstract is published; that counts." Her own standards are higher than the college's; she would write a book before applying for a full professorship. "Actually, I like the manageable level of the scholarly work. It keeps me from moving to a four-star school, since I want to keep time for a private life. I'd rather be good at my job at a less demanding school instead of struggling at a better school." St. Francis has a reputation for good teaching and Glascock would "rather turn out decently educated people than more data."

Glascock believes she has had more opportunities because of her several minority roles, including being a Protestant at a school steeped in Catholic traditions. Glascock suspects she was sometimes chosen for committees or conferences because she is a woman, and remarks that even her department office was a result of reverse sexism; the vice president for room assignments felt she might not be safe in an out-of-the-way cubbyhole, and so gave her a central spot. Being female helped in getting tenure, too, although Glascock does not suspect tokenism. She has a very good relationship with the dean and the president, and "when I say something, it's listened to."

Glascock complains about the school's elitist attitude toward liberal arts studies (as opposed to "the trades": health, accounting, and business courses). Despite the fact that the latter areas attract over half the students, all St.

Francis students must take 42 core credits of liberal arts courses. Psychology, computers, and language courses are not considered "liberal arts." Glascock also laments the students' parochialism. Though the college is situated in a pretty, historical residential neighborhood just across the bridge from a bustling business capital, "the students rarely go to the city, and dimly heard of the Vietnam War." Glascock's students are nearly all nurses and she cites lack of stimulation as the most serious negative in her job. "In my two women's classes, no one has ever considered herself a feminist!" Even though five departments are now headed by women, the faculty voted last year to return to the term "chairman." "Any change is fought. I proposed coteaching some interdisciplinary course, like 'Coping with Stress,' or 'Death and Dying,' which met with initial resistance.

While Glascock has come to terms with her salary, not all academics are content with their earnings potential. When Northeast Missouri State University paid Geraldine Ferraro $17,500 to speak on campus, one out-of-town newspaper griped that the fee nearly equaled the annual salary of an instructor with a master's degree!

College teaching positions have been scarce in recent years, with many Ph.D. holders unable to find suitable positions, or accepting meager salaries in undesirable locations or third-rate schools. There is good news ahead, though; by 1999, about 100,000 of the country's fulltime professors will retire. Faculty members hired when the baby-boom generation went to college have been there since the 1960s. College enrollments soared in the 1950s and 1960s, spurred by veterans studying on the G.I. bill, and later by the baby-boom children born just after World War II. The high school graduate population has been decreasing since 1979, but college enrollments will begin to rise again by the mid 1990s. For the immediate future, openings are likeliest in math and many science areas, foreign languages important for international relations (Russian and Chinese), and international studies (concentrating on the Far East or Middle East, for example).

By the mid to late 1990s, though, openings will occur in every academic field, including the arts, which have been particularly difficult recently. If you had set aside your dreams of academia, now is the time to resurrect them, so that, Ph.D. in hand, you can enter what promises to be an excellent job market as we near the year 2000.

College professors like their generous vacations and flexible schedules, providing ample time for travel and personal interests. The long summer off allows the opportunity to be a visiting professor at a different type of campus, elsewhere in America or in another country. This means additional earnings, too; faculty members are never lavishly paid. Many appreciate the vibrancy of a student community, and relish the stimulation of teaching bright, motivated young adults. The campus atmosphere or college-town setting can hold great appeal as well; consider all the alumni who linger on for years in Berkeley, Madison, or Austin.

All is not idyllic in academia, though. The "publish-or-perish" edict still governs at many universities, and newer professors may be assigned huge, impersonal lecture classes arranged for cost effectiveness rather than optimal learning conditions. With lower enrollments, colleges have been hard pressed financially, with faculty directly affected. Many talented instructors leave the field because they resent the low salary (often around $20,000) and see no chance to obtain tenure in their departments.

Held in high public esteem, university professors are interviewed and quoted in newspapers or on television; they are generally regarded as experts in their fields. You can find adjunct teaching positions at junior or community colleges with only a master's degree, and this is a fine way to test your enjoyment of the activity. It is extremely difficult to teach at a four-year institution without a Ph.D., a long and expensive undertaking. (The exceptions, of course, include prominent poets or novelists, invited to teach writing courses, or a brilliant corporate executive recruited by a graduate business school. If you are not famous, plan on a doctorate.)

SENIOR PROGRAM DIRECTOR FOR A NONPROFIT EDUCATIONAL ASSOCIATION

Phil Williams was a trainer and financial analyst for a major bank, where he trained staff in operations and international awareness until 1981. His next job was directing continuing education programs in finance at a local university. The American Management Association (AMA), where he now works, is "similar to a university, but national in scope. Our single major product is seminars, generating 60 percent of our revenue." Other sources of revenue are books and memberships. The AMA sends out millions of brochures each year.

Williams's division runs a fundamentals of finance course more than 50 times a year across the country, and offers 40 other seminars on topics such as cost accounting, cash management, and budgeting. Williams describes his own job as a project-manager role:

> I'm involved in marketing my seminars: defining the audience, suggesting and selecting mailing lists. I develop new products. [The] AMA has lots of group-think, but you're free to move in your own area. The job is entrepreneurial, with creative aspects. I fill out a form for new seminar ideas, then meet with the marketing people to discuss whether it will sell. We have to be profit-and-loss concious, concerned constantly with revenues and expenses.

Williams's division budget covers speakers, course materials, honoraria, word processing, and other overhead costs. The marketing department makes allocations for advertising and promotion. New seminars are tested in smaller cities first.

Williams's job at the bank was in a training area, too, but the context was quite different. "In a corporation, training is not a priority (except for the credit area in a bank), so there was less pressure to constantly produce. You responded to management's requests. Because is was fun, and not a profit center, it wasn't highly regarded." At the banks, training was part of the human resources area, which was subject to frequent cuts and was regarded as a staff department, providing a service. "Training is more hectic at [the] AMA than it was at the bank. If a speaker of mine gets sick, the customers may be upset. When it's an internal training program, you can say, 'Okay, folks, we have to postpone this program today. We'll do it next week.' They're not paying for it. Bank employees were generally there because they were sent. At AMA, seminars are not cheap; attendees really want to be here. They often arrive at 8:15 or 8:30 for a 9 A.M. session, and are eager to learn." Employers pay the fees for most AMA seminar participants.

Williams explains, "Program directors are recognized for success here. Rewards are not directly financial, but could be reflected in annual reviews. It's not a one-to-one relationship, though." The economy affects AMA enrollments very directly. Williams feels he would be earning more in banking at a similar job—perhaps as a second vice president with a thrift incentive plan to equal greater earnings. He gets 20 vacation and personal days each year, with good educational benefits. "AMA has a lower pay scale, similar to a university," Williams finds. "Benefit costs are rising so fast only profit-making companies can afford a generous package. Educational benefits such as tuition remission are good. The profit sector has cut back on tuition, and if you have kids, tuition remission can be a fabulous benefit."

Hours were easier at the bank, "because we weren't customer-responsive. If a project got postponed or cancelled, we just relaxed. At AMA, my hours are at least 9 to 5. Courses on the West Coast run until 8 P.M. EST, and I should be here to provide customer service. We need to be here as much as possible. You work harder," he concludes. Williams does not travel with his programs, and is not getting involved in what he calls "product-driven telemarketing."

What are the rewards? "More ability to control your own destiny. You can develop products that make money, and

The Program Department: Providing the Service   109

contribute to the organization. You *do* make a difference. I'm learning marketing and product development, acquiring diverse business experience. We look upon ourselves as the best. The organization depends on you for revenue. We have to make tough decisions. In a sense, you live and die with your programs. Certain trade-offs are made: we can run this program ten times a year and get 30 people, or 20 times and get 20 people. Do I have a market? Do I have an audience?" He finds the work more exciting than his previous jobs. "The burden is on you to create products that will get bought."

It helps in Williams's work to have a liberal arts background, in order to deal with people. He has two master's degrees, in economic history and European history. His technical knowledge was acquired in his operations experience at the bank, and by taking "lots of courses." He is currently trying to learn new skills, especially direct marketing and marketing psychology. The AMA is giving him experience in training, marketing, and general management.

Williams's job is representative of positions at many of America's more than 6,000 professional and trade associations. They frequently offer continuing educationl courses, conferences, and seminars for members. At organizations like the American Medical Association, the Modern Language Association, or the American Institute of Certified Public Accountants, program directors survey members, develop programs, and present them to professionals in the field. Conference planning is a key skill for these roles (or one that you will learn by having a job in this area), and it helps to have had direct experience in the industry you are assisting. Associations often prepare and disseminate printed information and publications for members (see Chapter 7).

Another activity these nonprofit associations may be involved in is lobbying. Based in Washington, D.C., or their own state capital, lobbyists must be very familiar with their subject and adept at gaining access to legislators and their staff members. It is a growing area in terms of employment, and special-interest groups make up a significant percentage of the 10,500 D.C. lobbyists. Generating public support and disseminating information to increase awareness is the second important concern of lobbyists. Those who lobby on behalf of big-business concerns are highly paid; public-interest lobbyists, of course, are at the lower end of the salary scale, starting out at around $20,000 to $25,000. A typical route to a lobbyist position is starting out with the professional group, learning its issues, and moving up to the Washington (or state) level.

CONSULTANT AT A FOUNDATION HELPING ARTS ORGANIZATIONS

Karen Schaeffer is the director of the theater program at the Foundation for the Extension and Development of American Professional Theater (FEDAPT). FEDAPT, a nonprofit management-consultant group, helps provide tools to theater and dance companies. Services include publications on key topics; national conferences; intensive invitation-only training institutes on marketing, fund raising, and fiscal controls; and one-to-one consulting by full-time professionals who spend a day or two with a group needing their skills. Supported by contributions, FEDAPT works with theaters in transition. Schaeffer recruits, selects, and assigns consultants, and then coordinates their efforts. She travels a great deal, evaluating programs at the site, and meeting with both consultant and theater staff.

FEDAPT analyses the need, determines the problems, and performs in-depth evaluations by telephone. Often, theater companies don't know exactly what they need. FEDAPT subsidizes the consulting services, and each company pays a portion of the costs. Schaeffer selects a suitable consultant for each project, with "skills, sensitivity, and a compatible personality. The consultant always leaves with some kind of 'action plan'—a homework assignment to the company." FEDAPT evaluates the commitment level of a company to determine how suitable the group will be for ongoing assistance, lasting up to two or three years. Management is always directed to ask their board of directors for monetary aid before FEDAPT helps them articulate goals. "We provide the tools so they can identify and research their own mission."

Schaeffer got her previous job with the Theater Communications Group through the state department of labor and sees her present role as a temporary new direction. She expects to return to arts management eventually and deal with day-to-day problems again. Of her current job, she says, "I can be phone friends with people I'd never get to meet. I get a good global view of what's happening in theater, from managers and development directors." While she does not particularly like the travel, she does get to see a great deal of theater, and remain up-to-date on what's happening in the American theater movement.

> I hear different opinions on how to do things in theater, since each company pursues its own mission. FEDAPT can help and get them to start talking. We have lively discussions about plays and audiences. Working for a service organization means helping people, feeling a part of making it happen. It's exciting. I don't have the crisis management of an online manager, but of course I also get secondhand satisfactions.

She feels the negatives of her work are "not going to the rehearsals, and not being there to see all the performances." FEDAPT is well known and well respected on the national performing arts scene, and Schaeffer seems to take pride in being so central in delivering its services to theater companies. Clearly, she feels deeply attached to the professional theater movement and thoroughly enjoys being a part of it. Consulting firms generally look for staff with some experience in the area, even at the beginning levels, so this cannot be the starting point for your career in the nonprofit world. It may be a reasonable goal for your second or third job in the arts world.

A larger layer of consulting firms helps the nonprofit community carry out its work. Many of the big consulting shops, providing services including fund raising, event planning, direct mail, or telemarketing, are for-profit businesses operating nationally. But within the 501(c)3 category are many small organizations set up to consult with not-for-profits, in public relations, technical assistance, fund raising, management, staff development, or new business ventures. Starting jobs may be as researchers or administrative assistants, which affords the opportunity to learn the work and gradually take on some staff responsibilities.

Nonprofit consulting groups for other nonprofits have to raise the money for their own operation in order to be able to provide their services at low or no cost. This means they have development directors, proposal requests, and budgetary constraints, just as their clients do. This is a small but interesting area of opportunity if you are deeply committed to the nonprofit community and its philosophy.

7

Membership and Publications

INTRODUCTION TO THE MEMBERSHIP DEPARTMENT

Not all nonprofits have members, of course. Hospitals, animal shelters, and social service agencies help patients and clients in times of need but do not expect them to join up as regular participants. For thousands of museums, historical societies, community development groups, unions, audience-sponsored broadcasting stations, social-action and environmental/preservation organizations, however, the membership department is the cornerstone of their activities. Imagine the Girls Scouts, the Sierra Club, or your local YMCA without members!

If you enjoy both public contact and detail work, membership is a logical area for you to explore. While you will not be the most visible worker in the organization, you will have the satisfaction of knowing the organization could not continue without the success of your efforts.

FUNCTIONS OF THE MEMBERSHIP DEPARTMENT

How do these key departments serve the nonprofits depending upon them? Ernest Hood, assistant manager for development and audience services at a member-supported radio station, summarizes his responsibilities as "getting new members, keeping them, and servicing them." His station's 38,000 members are tended by a full-time staff of five, plus three volunteers. On a smaller scale, a 123-year-old county historical society has grown from 900 to 1,500 members in the past year by revamping its image and launching direct-mail campaigns. The development director, assisted by a membership secretary, channels much energy towards building the society's membership base.

Program Director of a YMCA

Dawn MacNutt, program director of a YMCA in a gentrifying urban neighborhood, calls her employer "a service organization soliciting members." Local branches scale their fees to the community. MacNutt supervises the membership office, handling 3,000 dues payers. "The membership office is the front line in a small branch like this one," she explains. "It's a very integral part of the Y." Diverse office responsibilities include marketing, sales, sign up, and promotion of scheduled classes. The staff members sell guest passes, T-shirts, and swim caps; catalog all members on computer; send mailings; and issue photo identification cards to new members. They field gripes and questions, and try to make substitutions for filled classes.

The membership office is open from 9 A.M. to 8 P.M. daily and from 9 A.M. to 6 P.M. on weekends. It is staffed by a manager, two computer operators, and two desk clerks, who take turns for weekend work. The shifts are 9 A.M. to 3 P.M., or 3 P.M. to 8 P.M. When hiring staff for the membership office, MacNutt looks for people with financial knowledge to handle bookkeeping, receipts, logging, and tallies. Employees also need a good sense of humor, as the job involves a lot of contact with the public. "People arrive with the day's baggage, so the staff needs to defuse tense customers," says MacNutt. "You must laugh at yourself and your own mistakes, and present yourself in a pleasing manner. Personality is 60 percent of the job; we're selling. We're here to have members, not turn them away." She looks for low-key personnel who can learn details quickly.

Six months ago, MacNutt hired Arnold Richardson as membership manager. He found the job through a local newspaper ad. He had left his assistant vice president position at a community savings-and-loan association, which he found very stressful. "It was Ulcer City, U.S.A." Richardson enjoys public contact, especially with children, and hopes to do more for teenagers, who join "to have a place for gymnastics and basketball." Youth membership, he notes, has increased dramatically of late. His hours are 9 A.M. to 5 P.M., and he trains his own staff. "The regular season is hectic, with new courses starting every eight weeks. In between, we sign people up for memberships and make class changes, if, for example, a kid is in the wrong level swimming class," Arnold explains. He maintains a record of inquiries about classes the Y does not offer, like tennis or lifeguard training, and brings suggestions to the program staff.

Besides the skills his boss looks for, Richardson feels "tact and diplomacy are needed. No one likes to give or receive bad news, but our office has to solve problems including cancelled memberships or refunds." For instance, the need for strong interpersonal skills surfaced when, "a Muslim gentleman wanted a family membership—but he had three wives! We persuaded him to join with his children only."

For the office jobs, which entail constant contact with members, Richardson stresses the need for courtesy, clear judgment, and simple financial skills. His staff members handle money and credit cards, work out interest-free payment plans, and arrange monthly installments via electronic funds transfer. He emphasizes that "the key is to create a friendly atmosphere, make people comfortable coming here. I'd rather have people satisfied, leading to good word of mouth."

Assistant Manager at a Member-supported Radio Station

According to Ernest Hood, a radio station manager,

> In membership you're less involved in a particular project, but [more] concerned with people and perceptions of your programming, and their loyalty to the programs. The membership is your population, and you have a responsibility to them. I feel committed to the station and what we've promised our members: good radio, the kind of programs they've tuned in for. That's why they believe in us. We help make it mean more to be a member than just getting a nice program guide.

Hood, who has been at the station since January 1985, had been a listener before he answered its local newspaper ad. Since college, he has always worked in the nonprofit sector, and he took this job specifically to learn about membership activities. Previously, he was with a documentary film company, working on grants and reports. His current job involves supervising the membership office, and he admits to missing his writing somewhat. He helps out with the station's direct-mail solicitations and special mailings, and oversees the thank-you letters for larger donors ($100 or more). His department, like many membership offices, works closely with—in fact, shares offices with—the development staff, who select some of the larger contributors for further cultivation. While 38,000 subscribers might seem like a vast number for any nonprofit organization, it represents only 8 to 10 percent of this station's listeners, leaving ample room for growth.

The station sends four letters a year reminding each member to renew. Other mail campaigns seek extra contributions from current or lapsed members. Appeals are sent at the end of both the calendar and fiscal years, and for Valentine's Day or the first day of spring. The station also holds two on-air drives each year, for ten days each. If necessary, they will hold a charge-a-thon, accepting credit-card pledges only, "to get us immediate revenues if we're behind in our goals."

The station is trying to improve database management, and Hood is working on the transition to its new computer system, helping to determine the needs and meeting with the systems programmer. Reflecting the views of many nonprofits, he explains, "an essential part of membership is the data base, storing names, addresses, demographic data, and amount of gift. We hope, with our new computer, to be able to segment the audience by program preference to provide better, faster, and more direct service." The new computer will allow more personal appeals, so that a letter signed by the host of a popular program could be sent only to listeners of that program. "Members' motives," Hood finds, "are loyalty to the music or the particular radio personality, like Pegeen Fitzgerald or Garrison Keillor." He has a lot of phone contact with members, especially during on-air drives, when he and a colleague supervise volunteers who are on hand from 6 A.M. to midnight. A special party at the end of each drive thanks the volunteers, as many as 150 of whom work at an on-air drive each day. With an active volunteer pool of 500, Hood tries to figure out better ways to involve them. For instance, he would like to see the volunteers generate a special event.

Occasionally, members call with complaints such as a missing program guide or a late-arriving premium gift. Hood also visits the premium house to take part in choosing the mugs, tote bags, and other gifts for members. He manages the new discount program, another benefit for members, which he hopes will "integrate the station into the city's cultural fabric." He initiates contacts and makes arrangements for discounts at performing arts centers and record shops. As liaison to the station's computer house, he manages mailing-list rentals and exchanges as well. They send mailings to lists, which may lead to listeners, if not subscribers, immediately.

Hood agrees with Dawn MacNutt on the key skills for membership jobs, adding "patience, writing, scheduling, and record keeping. Be articulate and diplomatic; you may have to bend over backwards to say 'it's our fault.' " He underscores the importance of understanding how to use a computer system: "tracking is critical."

Hood spends most of his working day in the office and is on the phone a great deal, although setting up the discount program will keep him out more. His hours are 9 A.M. to 5 P.M. (longer during on-air drives), and his vacation time will increase from three weeks to four with seniority. Salaries are "better than in the past, and good for nonprofits." Beginners in the department start in the high teens. Hood cites a good benefits package, including major medical and dental care, overtime pay for nonmanagers, and compensatory time on an individual basis. The staff is currently being unionized. His station, a member of both the National Public Radio and American Public Radio, has a municipal license, issued to the city, which provides rent-free office space high in the Municipal Building. The glorious skyline views dazzle visitors, but Hood says staff members get used to it.

Membership Director at Asia Society

Tracey Ann Smith-Berg, who is in charge of membership at The Asia Society, cites their beautiful building and offices as two advantages. With a B.A. in dance and psychology, Smith-Berg's goal has been arts management, which proved a difficult quest. An employment agency sent her to The Asia Society, where she was hired as a research assistant. "I loved it," she recalls. "All I did was read. I found potential sources of funds, researched backgrounds of trustees, assisted in the capital campaign for our new building, and worked on the twenty-fifth anniversary dinner." She stayed for one year. When she returned from two years in Brazil with her spouse, a banker who had been assigned to Latin America, the society offered a raise and promotion.

Smith-Berg's job now involves keeping the 6,600 members across America who provide $300,000 each year and increasing the membership base. She designed and wrote direct-mail pieces, sent to 78,000 people in 1984, and called them effective. With offices in Houston, Washington, and New York, the society runs round-table discussions, corporate meetings, and press conferences to educate Americans about Asia. Other offerings include a performing arts program featuring Asian troupes, touring exhibits, publications and panels for businesspeople, a journal for social studies teachers, educational video tapes, and film screenings.

Smith-Berg arranges members-only film screenings, as well as some performance and gallery openings. She writes invitations, prepares a calendar of events, maintains a mailing list, and oversees an assistant. As the development associate for individual members, she is part of an active office staff of seven, which works closely and shares space with the two-person public relations department. Her time is spent

> writing a lot, and talking to members all the time. I arrange three yearly openings for 1,000 members, from 10 A.M. to 10 P.M., coordinating refreshments, music, and volunteers. These include special members' previews, for donors of $200 or more. R.S.V.P. for members-only events is by phone, providing very individualized attention. I get ethnic restaurants to participate in events, draft letters to prospective members, and answer requests for information about Asia Society.

The society is currently shifting to a more efficient database system. "Volunteers type and file, which helps a lot, and so does our work-study student." Involved in the organization's new ad campaign, Smith-Berg suggested response coupons to generate membership. She works closely with other departments, submits membership lists for the society's annual report, and monitors mailings to keep a reasonable flow.

Smith-Berg's hours are normally 9 A.M. to 5 P.M., with one

late evening each month. Because she lives in a suburb an hour away, she delegates evening film screenings. "Asia Society is gracious about scheduling, if you get your work done," Smith-Berg remarks, reflecting a common attitude in nonprofits. She appreciates the benefits, particularly a staff development fund that finances tuition or travel activities for employee enrichment. She plans a trip to Japan, Hong Kong, and China with her husband in 1986. She must submit an itinerary and work-related goal for a two-week (or longer) trip to qualify for the $2,000 allowance. According to Smith-Berg, "Lots of the staff use this benefit, and meet with performers in the home countries." The society likes employees to have some Asian background; Smith-Berg had been an exchange student in Japan one summer. The Asia Society runs tours, escorted by a staff member and expert in the area. The professional staff get to travel, mostly internationally, and often to Washington, D.C.

The advantages of Smith-Berg's job include "high standards for employees; all associates have college degrees. It's an articulate, high-level staff. We entertain Asian dignitaries, like the Queen of Thailand, the Dalai Lama, and prime ministers. It's an interesting environment, with lots of exposure." She also appreciates having Fridays off in July and August and likes "all the variety and autonomy. No one looks over my shoulder, and there's no time clock. I keep learning new skills. People are friendly, easy to work with. I enjoy having goals to meet and taking risks." She likes watching their new building grow; they now own the prime-location land on which the building stands and have no mortgage, leaving the organization "more stable, debt-free, with a balanced budget. The four-year transition phase meant cost cutting for a while, with reduced benefits to members, and higher charges, lids on raises, and a hiring freeze. *Asia Magazine* folded. We were besieged on all sides; it was tough," she recalls. "Now we're more secure. You know your paycheck will be there."

On the negative side, Asia Society, like many other nonprofits, has no endowment; a new Challenge grant, hopefully, will create one. Smith-Berg also cites "high turnover, due to low pay, which cuts into commitment." High turnover also means no stagnation; however, she's reported to "three different development directors, with three distinct styles, so the job has changed, too." She does not like the office politics, lack of advancement opportunity, or limited earnings. However, she acknowledges, "I don't want a consuming job. More responsibility and more hours would mean more money, taking time away from my modern dance activities, entertaining, and social life."

Historical Society Director

Although Lorraine Slater's title is development director of a county historical society, much of her work revolves around building the membership. With a bachelor's degree in English literature, Slater spent six years in printing sales before joining the local zoo to work on direct mail, followed by a proposal-writing job at the National Audubon Society. A friend told her about the historical society's opening. With a new executive director revamping its image, the society's staff has grown from seven to 20 within the past three years. Now beginning her second year, Slater remembers:

> I started from scratch, with a very old organization that's developed a new image. I came from a national mailing program. Whose [mailing] lists could we use here? The other cultural institutions and local newspaper subscription lists were obvious. I tried the phone book for other leads. Now we're branching out to other community newspapers. It's fun exploring the possibilities.

Her first task, developing membership, required identifying the constituency. A small direct-mail campaign, funded by a foundation, got a 2 percent response. Membership has grown 60 percent this year, with 600 new members in the past few months. Another mailing, written by Slater, who also works with designers, will be sent very soon. "We're hoping for more members through special exhibits, like our baseball memorabilia show. Our small exhibit space will be renovated and expanded. We're also trying to contact relocated natives." The organization now mails 55,000 pieces annually.

Slater finds her writing background very useful, and "sales experience helped me say things persuasively." The skills Slater feels are valuable for membership work, besides writing, are interpersonal ability, a flair for presentation, and the ability to organize diverse projects and handle varied responsibilities. She, too, stresses the need for computer literacy, and recommends courses in marketing, writing, and psychology as a good basic background.

The best part of the job, for Slater, is "making a difference; the satisfaction I get from seeing the organization develop; finding the people to whom it appeals; presenting a situation to a new person, striking a spark of interest, and watching them make a commitment to the organization." Her hours are the usual 9 A.M. to 5 P.M., and Slater calls her salary "good; fair compared to the organization's budget. Benefits in nonprofit are especially good, with generous vacation time. The benefits package has increased considerably since I've been here."

Though Slater did not mention it, we were struck by the beautiful work setting. The Society is housed in a gracious old brownstone on a lovely tree-lined street near the river. With rapid expansion, office space has been created in odd nooks, so both Slater and the public relations director work in corners of the balcony above the research library. If you like rare books, woodwork, unusual surroundings, and turn-of-the-century architecture, this would be an ideal environment.

Membership Director at Performing Arts Center

Amy Schancupp, another membership director, has worked for the past three years in a classic 1906 building for America's oldest performing arts center. She describes her department's main tasks as "raising money, accounting, tracking, acknowledgments, and keeping donors happy." Schancupp serves as a "patron desk," meaning that any member can call her with requests or responses to invitations. She arranges seven open rehearsals a year, sending invitations to all members two weeks beforehand. She meets donors at the rehearsals, welcomes and shepherds them to seats, and keeps them out of the front orchestra if performers request empty rows. Two months in advance, Schancupp begins working out the details of an open rehearsal with performers, ushers, and other staff members.

After receiving a bachelor's degree in theater, Schancupp worked for a publisher, a rock music booking agency, and then volunteered at various theater companies for a year in her spare time, helping with a newsletter to get useful experience for her job hunt and references. She sent a letter and resume to a number of arts organizations, seeking an entry-level job, and then followed up with phone calls, using *Art Search* (a biweekly job newsletter) for leads. When the Academy of Music needed an administrative assistant, she was contacted. For the first four months, she states, "I learned assorted word processors. Then the membership director moved to marketing, and I got the job." Now Schancupp has an assistant, a graduate student at a local college whose neighbor works at the academy. "Fred is neat, meticulous, the opposite of me," she laughs. "He has an M.A. in acting, so he may stay here," she adds.

Membership is part of the planning and development department, and Schancupp works to get both new members and renewals. The department uses a "house list" to try to convert ticket buyers to members. For renewals, they contact people who last contributed a year ago, and they are experimenting with letters, phone calls, and combinations of the two. Now that the entire organization is on a sophisticated computer system, Schancupp's work is easier. The computer generates acknowledgments, stores information, and writes thank-you notes, receipts, and reports. If Schancupp wants to know who has stopped contributing, the computer will print out information from any recent year and locate past donors. New members can choose premiums, which she helps select. She meets with suppliers, arranging for items such as records by artists who have performed at the academy. She has found, though, that "donors like intangibles best—things like the best seats or invitations to open rehearsals." All members get news of rehearsals and of subscription series, plus cast parties, receptions, and other special events, which Schancupp attends.

Schancupp writes the copy for different types of mailings, also, and prepares a list for professional telemarketers to use for phone solicitations. She begins planning the "acquisitions" mailing in late summer, to be sent out early in December, a traditional "giving season." Schancupp chooses the concept and artists; the in-house art department does layout and design, while she revises, proofreads, and supervises the packet, watching over the printing and mail-house phase. The academy mails 100,000 pieces. The hours, Schancupp reports, "get very busy." She often works longer than 9 A.M. to 5 P.M. and expects to be around all day on Saturdays for the seven open rehearsals, when "there's a lot of detail—large coffee urns, printed rehearsal passes." What does it take to execute all these tasks? "Attention to detail! Numbers, or at least knowing where to get them. Record keeping and coding. Writing well. Flexibility, so you can move from mail to telemarketing. Phone contact, which may be in spurts, during a phone-a-thon or rehearsals. Computer or word-processing fearlessness," Schancupp summarizes.

The best parts of her job are that she is now computer literate, gets to write, and is involved in contemporary performing arts. "I get to see as many performers as possible, and learn about music." Benefits are standard, with a two-week vacation, plus good medical and dental insurance. During their performance season, staff work some holidays, which is then added to vacation time. As for negatives, Schancupp cites "long hours, but comp time is available, flexible. Pay is low, like all the arts. If you stick at it long enough, you'll make a living wage—I do. I'd rather be doing something I like."

INTRODUCTION TO THE PUBLICATIONS DEPARTMENT

Most nonprofits produce some sort of written materials, most frequently brochures and annual reports. In organizations relying heavily on publications for reputation or revenue, one or more full-time staff positions are created to produce them. Very well known, well established periodicals, like *Smithsonian* or *Natural History*, have full-fledged staffs of their own, with art directors, advertising managers, editors, and circulation supervisors. We have elected to examine the more typical publications jobs in the not-for-profit world, ranging from a small community newsletter to a glossy series of renowned handbooks.

FUNCTIONS OF THE PUBLICATIONS DEPARTMENT

Editor of *Peoples Firehouse*

Albina Jackanin, who edits the *Peoples Firehouse* monthly newsletter, has lived in the stable urban working-class neighborhood since 1936 and joined the community organization 11 years ago. The folksy, small-town-type periodical is 12 to 16 pages long. It helps publicize the organization's activities and sell tickets to such events as a fund-raising brunch or a tenth anniversary celebration. Jackanin collects news and information from other local groups, and residents bring her additional items. She scans the mass media for news of interest to her readers and refers to past issues for her column of birthday wishes and expressions of sympathy. A Ford Foundation grant supports the publication, which is distributed free in the neighborhood. Circulation is 3,000, with 710 copies mailed to 34 states and overseas. "Getting articles from staff is the hardest part," she says with a smile.

Her tasks include layout, typing articles, handling calendar information, and assigning articles. The local community board provides a monthly article. She responds to occasional inquiries from readers and sprinkles little quotes from magazines and newspapers to fill small spaces. Volunteers collate copies, and Peoples Firehouse pays for offset. Jackanin delivers the newsletters, helped by seven volunteers, to stores along the main streets and to local churches, which puts her in contact with community residents. Classified ads are free (donations are welcome), and merchants make a contribution in exchange for a display ad; these contributions help pay bulk postage costs. Jackanin, who is fairly artistic, inherited the bulletin when the previous editor moved. A local resident designed and donated the logo—two fire hydrants. Jackanin goes to most community meetings, where residents share news and report upcoming local events.

"Sometimes I'm here till 10 P.M.," says Jackanin. "Other times, the hours are normal." Compensatory time is available, and Jackanin enjoys evening work. "My children and my husband are gone. I live around the corner, and the bulletin is my baby. If I didn't love it, I wouldn't do it."

Jeff Decy, a young colleague, proofreads and fills in, in case of illness. He "converts contributed works into standard English" and also edits a newsletter for the local merchants association, which goes to 100 retailers. An English major in college, Jeff is now the director of economic development at Peoples Firehouse, and he meets with the local manufacturers' board about security programs. He plans to produce some new publications, such as a directory of merchants or a directory of industries. His employer has a contract with the city for commercial revitalization, providing help with seeking grants and business promotion. Twenty-three stores received capital assistance and free help with design projects, including new signs or storefronts. Decy visits every community store.

Industry is mostly "low tech," Decy reports, with many firms in furniture, paper, printing, textile or apparel, and metal-stamping. Business is expanding, due to high rents in more glamorous parts of the city. Because 14,000 people enter the area each day for factory jobs in 780 businesses, in addition to the 7,000 local residents, Decy plans to start a newsletter for the growing community. The majority of the

Peoples Firehouse staff live in the neighborhood, and several other professionals are trying to find homes in the waterfront district.

Communications Director at an Artists Guild

Communications Director Margi Trapani is similarly dedicated to the community she serves at the Graphic Artists Guild. "I love the things the Guild represents and our issues. We're member-oriented, so I get to work with a lot of people. It's very diverse, constantly changing. I'm not slotted into doing the same things over and over. With filmscripts, newsletters, presswork, the tasks may be the same, but the dynamics of each group are different," she says.

A former fine arts major, Trapani has been at the Guild for four years. Previously, she painted and did promotional writing to earn extra money. "I have a varied resume. I never devoted full time to painting, but always sort of split between work with people and areas where there's a cause or meaningful social situation, which painting doesn't provide. The Guild synthesizes my talents." Her job originated when the executive director, aware of her efforts for another nonprofit, asked Trapani to do some volunteer work. Membership had just doubled, and Trapani soon became a part-time staff member for six months. "As the Guild grew by leaps and bounds, the need for communication services expanded." The Guild has 5,000 members now. Trapani works for the national office and serves as in-house consultant to the nine local chapters. She is managing editor of the monthly national newsletter, prepares membership literature, and edits *Pricing and Ethical Guidelines*, which is sold in major bookstores and revised every two years. Trapani says of her job:

> We all work as a team on Guild projects. When the membership director has a traveling workshop, I write the materials. I help with press and publicity for our executive director,

who works with legislators. I just produced a manual for our local chapters, outlining programs in different areas, orienting them to resources and services.

The Guild often gets requests for interviews or articles in trade publications. Trapani makes sure each article "is in Guild style, and well edited." She briefs board members for interviews, "helping them organize their facts and thoughts beforehand."

As a union, the Guild is supported by dues and revenues from their publications. It interacts with other organizations about mutual issues. "The executive director often speaks elsewhere, and I might go along to a local organization, where we teach them how to run a smooth meeting, recruit, and delegate responsibility. We'll help groups set up phone banks to reach members about an event; I'll write a script for them. "

"Much of the work here has to do with how a message is relayed," Trapani believes. "Members are our best recruiters. We have an artist-to-artist hotline, for direct help with problems, plus workshops on negotiating, self-promotion, and taxes, which have brought visibility and new members." Trapani publicizes the workshops and helps new leaders learn to communicate well. "It's because member activities always have a communications aspect that my job is so varied," she explains. Trapani stresses the importance of working with the graphic designer. "I explain the image we want to project. I need a good idea of how a designer works, and must be as articulate as possible about the effect I want so the designer can communicate it visually."

The national staff consists of the executive director, a membership services and education director, Trapani, an administrative assistant, and part-time interns from a nearby art school. Trapani spends 60 percent of her time writing and editing, the other 40 percent on conversations and coaching. "It varies with how much help the chapters need. Some weeks I'm doing press releases, some weeks [I'm] on the phone a lot." Publications receiving releases can call her, or she them, to explain things more fully or get additional information.

Trapani's hours are 10 A.M. to 6 P.M. and meetings are usually at night; she attends three to six evening meetings a month. The whole staff goes to monthly board meetings.

> It's a lot of work. Part of the fun of a small staff is you do get the diversity. It's easy to see where you fit into the organization. Teamwork is really exciting, when you each have an area of expertise and also work together. It's like a puzzle. We're all constantly learning. Our members teach us a lot. I get more autonomy in my own area than I'd have in a "normal" 9-to-5 job; that's a big plus.

One drawback Trapani cites is the lack of resources. "You see what *could* be done, but must be very creative, without the funds to fly out to a local that needs help. In nonprofits, things sometimes take longer because you don't have the staff or resources."

Trapani also discusses the pros and cons of her relatively low salary.

> Obviously, I could make more money in the corporate world. Working for something I believe in is very important. I do think about the money. The Guild and similar organizations try to come as close as they can to other salaries but will never match corporate levels. As long as I feel the organization cares about its employees, it's worth it. I've worked in the corporate world and didn't feel as involved or useful. I don't like the feeling of spending my workday totally on someone else's priorities, or on things that don't really matter to me. There's never a time where you have to think of what to do."

According to Trapani, the most important skills for her job are writing clearly and editing well. She also notes that

> you have to work with people, in groups and individually, and help translate their needs and issues for readers who aren't involved in our industry. Avoid jargon and don't be esoteric.

She encourages the members to write for the newsletter, stating

> since artists aren't writers, I have to help them get thoughts into written form, which takes skill. Sometimes, I'll interview the artist. It's fun. You have to understand what touches people, how they'll relate. You have to be a good listener, flexible, and well organized. You deal with a lot of interests. [You must] initiate—many people are involved, but no one tells you what you should be doing. The executive director and the board oversee, and new ideas can come from members, but you have to be thinking of improvements and new strategies.

As an active lobby, the Guild responds to issues affecting members, such as the copyright laws that led to a legislative proposal on the effects of new technologies. Trapani "translates and edits the executive director's paper, presenting the Guild position to the outside world." She also testified at the Office of Technological Assessment, a research arm of Congress. After the hearings, Trapani wrote press releases, newspaper articles, and material for other trade publications. "Legislation is a big educational tool for us," she points out.

Editor for Planned Parenthood

Educational tools are what Senior Editor Joanna Pugni produces for the Planned Parenthood Federation. She writes and researches four or five brochures each year and revises most of the 45 existing pamphlets annually. These brochures, 8 to 15 pages in length, are often distributed by other family-planning sources, including counselors, teachers, and agencies. The vice president for medical affairs updates Pugni's copy. "I translate medical prose into lay language. It's tricky not to sacrifice the medical accuracy but write for the consumer. I try to get away from a hard clinical tone as much as possible," Pugni explains. Some publications are also translated into Spanish.

Ten years ago, Pugni started as a staff writer at Planned Parenthood Federation, the national headquarters for nearly 200 affiliates. She has a B.A. in English literature, research and writing abilities, and previous publishing experience, editing magazines for small businesses. Although she claims "when you're a writer, you're a writer," her reasons for shifting from publishing for profit were personal. "The brochures really help people, educate, and may make their lives better. I seek the humanitarian nuance." Her job is very different from a similar job in a publishing company.

In magazines, a free-lancer sent me the article I'd assigned, and that was it. My publication went on newsstands every two months, leaving no time for multilayered comments on every sentence. Here, my work is done by committee. The new AIDS brochure will go to the vice president and 12 executive staff, who all make comments on the manuscript. I then integrate all the comments into the publication. A brochure here generally takes three months to produce. Planned Parenthood has one production person. We have an in-house graphic designer; other artwork is free-lanced, and I have input.

The skills required for her job are the same ones required in the profit sector. Pugni adds, however, that "you must have some kind of altruistic bent." She thinks her salary is satisfactory—she makes as much as she would as an editor at a publishing company. She appreciates the one-month vacation, pension plan, and tax-sheltered annuity, but misses bonuses, stock options, and profit sharing.

The 9 A.M. to 5 P.M. hours increase prior to annual meetings. Pugni prepares fact sheets, promotional materials (flyers and direct mail pieces to professional groups who use the brochures), and articles for the house organ. She hires freelance writers for special projects and annual reports. "There's an edge to the profit world that's missing here. We're more casual about deadlines and generally less pressured, although incorporating 12 people's comments is a kind of pressure." The rewards? Personal satisfaction, says Pugni. "The work is hard, with everything done by committee. You must cope with a lot of different personalities internally. We're insulated and isolated from the patients, but I get an occasional letter from a reader." Feedback comes through questionnaires sent to educators who use the pamphlets. Pugni is still interested in health topics, after a decade of involvement, but would not mind moving beyond family planning.

Director of Publications for a Botanical Garden

The opportunity to edit *Plants and Gardens*, the most prestigious publication in botany, lured Barbara Pesch to her current job. The daughter of a landscape architect, she grew up in a Midwestern plant nursery and earned a B.S. in botany. She worked for Sunset Books and volunteered at the Chicago Botanical Garden, a job that turned into a paid position. After a stint at the Missouri Botanical Garden, Pesch relocated three years ago to become director of publications at a well-reputed, 76-year-old urban botanical garden. She walks to work, admits she probably puts in more hours because she lives nearby, and likes the camaraderie of a small not-for-profit. "It's kind of like a family, with security, and a lot of pride among staff in what we do."

Editing and critiquing the 45-year-old series of quarterly handbooks requires horticultural training. Pesch chooses the topics for each year's handbooks, then selects and monitors a guest editor for each one. There are 15 to 18 contributors per handbook, and she oversees editorial and production work, hires a graphic artist, and checks galleys as they come back. Like the *Plants and Gardens* series, some booklets on special subjects are reprinted and sold nationally and internationally. Over 60 titles are in print, each consisting of compiled articles. All Garden members receive the quarterly handbooks and newsletters, also prepared by Pesch's department. The department prints 22,000 copies of each new *Plants and Gardens* title; successful sellers are reprinted. Some titles are perennials; pamphlets about herbs, propagation, orchids, and water gardens sell up to 12,000 copies each year, at $2.25 a copy.

Pesch's assistant, Bill Mulligan, does copy editing, clerical tasks, some rewriting (because experts in the field do not necessarily write well), and prepares manuscripts for publication. Mulligan was a free-lance writer with an agent and four published books, including two on gardening. He needed a regular income, however, and a part-time job opened up at the garden. He had edited the magazine *Popular Gardening Indoors* and his background impressed Pesch, who looks for "willingness to do clerical tasks and correspondence, write press releases for each new handbook, and mail review copies, plus get and return photos. Detail and follow-through are important." Noting his typing and filing skills, Mulligan observes, "my willingness to do clerical tasks, although it was far below what I was used to as a journalist, got me this job." He initially worked part-time, three days a week, for five months. When the garden put up an exhibit at the city flower show, Mulligan put in 18-hour days there, and believes this, combined with his desire and commitment, led to his full-time position. One advantage of working for a small organization is the chance to do things beyond your job description, such as Bill's exhibition idea, included in the flower show. "There are fewer bodies," he explains. "When something big is taking place, everyone's needed. You wear many hats."

Though their hours are technically 9 A.M. to 4:30 P.M., "the job has to get done. You get involved in other activities," like the Japanese Festival at cherry blossom time, the editors report. They often work weekends, for which they get compensatory time. Mulligan adds, "You feel the cause you work for is more gratifying than working on a product. You work towards some sort of good for people. And you're in a beautiful place." Both Mulligan and Pesch agree that their salaries are not as high as they would be in the corporate world, but "the arrival of unions to the garden has raised salary and benefits for everybody," Pesch observes. Mulligan comments, "Nonprofits always hide behind the sanctuary of limited funds in salary discussions. You never really know if the limits are a philosophy or a reality. Staff members are expected to work for less than corporate salaries because it's always been that way. Publishing, a glamour field, treats people that way, too."

Staff members are welcome to take courses the Garden offers to the public, but they usually do not have the time. One benefit Pesch appreciates is the chance to lead one members' trip a year, to sites like Alaska or Ireland, for about two weeks. Groups average 25 participants, accompanied by a travel agent. Pesch writes the mailings for the tours she will lead, after doing a "dry run" to plan the itinerary. "That comes out of vacation time; the actual tour is part of the work load. It's a lot of responsibility. You work 18 hours a day on a trip and must have horticultural knowledge to answer all of the questions." Regular vacation schedules are two weeks the second year and one month after five years.

The publications staff helps other professionals with editing and production needs. They publicize the events arranged by the public relations office, for example. A third publications writer, Betsy Kissam, whose background includes editing, writing, newspapers, and publishing experience, prepares the quarterly newsletter, press releases, and brochures. She writes the bimonthly members' mailing and all invitations to openings of art shows or events. Working closely with the horticultural staff, she compiles a weekly list, "What's In Bloom," for visitors, and four seasonal lists each year. The membership office and a mailing house handle the mechanics of sending all these materials, although the publications office keeps its own list of press people and contributors to their handbooks. "We're close to being computerized, which would help a lot," say Pesch. The marketing department handles distribution and catalog sales of the books.

Apart from the exhilaration of strolling through one of

America's most beautiful gardens to get to the office, the most striking feature of this publications staff is how much they like their work and surroundings.

Publications contribute strongly to the image of the organization. They may be all your contributors actually see of your group. For example, many subscribers to the *Smithsonian* magazine read the periodical each month, but rarely if ever get to visit the sprawling museum in Washington.

Public Relations

INTRODUCTION

For a nonprofit organization, public relations can attract new members, encourage contributions, raise community awareness of the programs and services available, and inspire current members to participate more actively. Through publicity and promotion efforts, the agency may win public support for its causes and concerns, or clarify misunderstandings about its work. At its most effective, a thoughtful public relations program establishes and maintains a positive image for the nonprofit group.

All of these accomplishments take place within an often limited budget, employing a variety of methods. Nonprofits use press releases, feature stories, photographs, press conferences, newsletters, brochures, and public speaking formats to communicate their message. Letters to the editor are a strong, cost-free method for keeping the organization in the public eye; radio and television appearances by top-level staff are another. The mass media provide free public service announcements to the nonprofit community, and the Advertising Council prepares topflight campaigns for organizations operating nationally. Special events are another method of publicizing the organization.

Many small nonprofit organizations do not have a public relations department, or even a specialist. Instead, the public relations functions are incorporated into another department, usually fund raising or membership. Nonetheless, this is a key function for any nonprofit, whether or not they can afford a full-time, exclusive position in the budget. "Public relations is the vehicle for successful fund raising," claims Jack Rimalover, vice president for resource development and public relations at a prestigious hospital. "Without a strong image perpetuated by public relations, you can't have effective fund raising or attract the best doctors and staff." In its community relations capacity, Rimalover's department runs a storefront that disseminates health information and assorted brochures. Besides the free materials, the storefront offers Telmed, a service that provides the public with audiotapes on particular topics, such as stress or insomnia.

PUBLIC RELATIONS AT A UNIVERSITY

Sara Gilbert has a classic public relations job at a large private university, where she promotes their continuing education offerings. Her responsibilities include preparing press releases, staging events, putting together "clipbooks" (compilations of publicity about the university), developing radio and television contacts, and answering questions from the press. "The university is a resource," she explains. "When you hear an academic expert quoted on T.V., he's there because the university public relations officer gave the networks a list. This helps the university. The press is beginning to learn what [areas] we have experts in, such as our real estate faculty." Three times a year, Gilbert sends a massive mailing of press releases announcing new programs for summer, winter, or spring terms, in an attempt to generate feature articles. She maintains a mailing list and is pleased that some of her releases are used nearly verbatim. Gilbert also sends listings to the calendar sections of various publications and creates "pitch letters" aimed at getting newspapers interested in writing articles about a course or program. Such stories can often be pegged to an event like "Adult Learning Week." She also tries to cultivate free-lance writers, encouraging them to use university resources—and, of course, mention their sources.

"Community relations and publicity are important to the university in two aspects: getting students to come and letting the community know about our services. We have a product to sell—education—and we want to make ourselves look like nice guys," Gilbert summarizes. She gets staff support, plus help from part-time employees and work-study students. Gilbert says of her job:

> It has a lot of nitty-gritty. I stuff envelopes, deal with the "Today" show, and paste little pieces of paper on bigger pieces of paper. I never do the same thing every day. To write press releases, I have to know about 45 different areas, from computers to real estate, and then create a headline and first paragraph to attract attention.

Gilbert finds that her job is very compatible with her professional goals. She notes that "public affairs people are smart and funny, and the atmosphere is easygoing." She is allowed to continue her free-lance writing though she cannot write for other colleges. And she has the advantage of "a great research facility—an outstanding library ten feet away, for lunch-hour research, that I wouldn't have access to otherwise." She likes the diversity her job offers, as well as the environment and the flexible schedule. She also appreciates the free tuition for herself and her family, and university housing priced dramatically below prevailing rates.

Gilbert claims she got to her current post by accident.

> When I was living in Maryland and writing, I wanted to get involved in the community. I visited local organizations to

do volunteer work in writing or public relations. This led to a half-time job in writing/public relations at a nearby community college. Upon relocating, I was free-lancing and writing books. Billing myself as "Editorial Specialist in College Public Relations" brought some free-lance work at the university.

Soon she was hired full time.

While she enjoys her job, Gilbert does cite some drawbacks. "Academic tradition means you can't rise above a certain point without a graduate degree. I'd have had to go to school for six more years to get a graduate degree for a $19,000 job at another university." She does take workshops and seminars on campus, but does so out of personal interest rather than for professional advancement.

"The budget's never there for adequate help," she regrets. She would like more assistance "and my own personal computer—pipe dreams." What would she look for in an assistant? "Common sense, articulateness, and great ability to deal with people. You must learn how to get what you need from others, and think on your feet with your mouth open. You need self-confidence and must be able to make a definite statement, organize, and coordinate mailings."

DIRECTOR OF COMMUNICATIONS AT A TEACHERS' UNION

Caring about the cause they work for is as important to public relations specialists as it is to any other nonprofit professionals. For Naomi Spatz, deputy director of communications for the United Federation of Teachers (UFT), the best part of her job is "working on something you really think makes a difference. In education, we can get pretty pretentious and feel we're affecting the future of society. We convince legislators, get a ground swell of popular support for something that will have a good impact. It's very satisfying." While Spatz believes public education is the underpinning of American society, she also feels that "education has become a rigid system, demeaning for professionals, who are treated worse than factory workers. We have to explain over and over why teachers need unions." The UFT, an 85,000-member local chapter of the nationwide American Federation of Teachers, is also organizing in higher education. They have already succeeded in raising the entry-level pay for teachers, Spatz claims with pride. "So much of the union's work is in political action, and what goes on in a classroom is affected by state and national laws," she states. With the prestigious Carnegie Commission now recommending the same changes Spatz wants to see in education, she is optimistic about the future of the field. She says one of her department's goals is "to attract and keep middle-class kids in local public schools." Another is to draw and keep talented professionals in the teaching field. A third is to inform the public about what happens in the schools.

Spatz, who believes strongly in her work at the United Federation of Teachers, sees her job as both internal and external communications. Her department keeps in touch with 85,000 local members through pamphlets, brochures, newsletters, and testimony for hearings on educational policy or funding at city, state, and national levels. Spatz is the voice of their "Hotline," a number members call for daily bulletins. She writes the copy, circulates it to other offices, and talks to members who have newsworthy ideas. Members are encouraged to call with tidbits about "good programs." External tasks include dealing with the press and "answering calls about bad news. We provide info to the public, especially the media, on UFT positions; arrange press conferences and press packets; find people for the press to interview on radio, television, or magazines. Topics range from bilingual education to Rap Rock: can it be part of a curriculum?" Spatz draws on a solid network; 1,000 local schools each have a chapter chairperson. Many magazines call requesting sources, and, like Sara Gilbert, Spatz helps track them down.

When hiring, Spatz looks for resourcefulness and interest in both education and the labor movement. Many UFT staff were teachers, and some of the communications personnel taught before moving to journalism. "Unions generally have members or field workers who move to staff jobs. The UFT is special," Spatz believes, "because 90 percent of our members are college graduates, with Ph.D.s in every imaginable field. It's useful to have a feel for the job whose members you represent." Some of their college interns get jobs upon graduation.

Asked about her hours, Spatz laughs and says, "we can work as much as we want—seven days, 12 hours [a day] if we like. When your project is in the headlines, you work hard. It's semiseasonal; schools are closed in the summer, and the office closes on school holidays. You can take four weeks' vacation." Spatz's usual hours are 10 A.M. to 6 or 7 P.M.

With a B.A. in labor relations, Spatz found all her jobs by networking. When she ran the AFL-CIO Committee for the United Nations, its board included local labor leaders acting as hosts to foreign dignitaries, offering the courtesies of the city. Spatz's strong international interests were welcome, as the committee paid special attention to newly independent nations. On the board was the UFT president, who Spatz briefed for his trip to Africa. When he heard she was leaving her job, the local president invited her to join the UFT. Because all her experience had been in international and national affairs, she declined; the labor leader pursued her for three months with ascending offers. Finally, in 1973, she accepted a job as assistant to the president, who had been eager to have Spatz's special knowledge of labor, the labor movement, and international affairs. Today, she retains her international ties by meeting with foreign visitors who want to learn about American education.

PUBLIC AFFAIRS IN AN ARTS MUSEUM

People come to public relations from many different backgrounds: Naomi Spatz was in labor relations, Jack Rimalover in for-profit marketing, Jim Meeuwsen a minister, and Sara Gilbert a free-lance writer. Susan Rapalee was a painter before joining the department of public affairs at an arts museum with a $9.5 million budget and 2 million objects in its vast collections. She came to the museum three years ago, as an administrative assistant in the director's office, and moved to public affairs after a year and a half to assist the public relations director. As a public institution receiving 50 percent of its operating funds from city government, the museum is asked to make space available to community groups at very low fees. Rapalee works on corporate and community receptions and sets up all of the internal arrangements for outside events held at the museum. She helped plan the 125th anniversary black-tie party to which a nearby medical school invited 750 guests, by working with the caterer, security, operations, and curatorial personnel. Community events keep Rapalee busy; her department maintains a master calendar for space in the museum, and other staff have to check with her to avoid conflicts. She coordinates with the education department about school groups, taking care to dovetail all events.

Rapalee's job does not entail much writing. (This has changed since our interview, however.) Her department will adapt articles from the curator's newsletter for a public-relations format. The museum director's office helps prepare press releases, sent to those on a mailing list of 1,100. An "A list," for whom Rapalee's department types labels, receives photographs. A mailing house and computerized labels are used for larger mailings; with more computers, the museum will soon be able to keep lists in-house and current.

The public affairs department also publicizes exhibitions and follows up afterward. They function as their own clipping service, culling news items and circulating them. "The routine of getting our press info is daily: order the labels, get photos, maintain mailing lists, see that releases are printed and edited," Rapalee notes. "We average 50 written or phoned requests for printed material each month, and 150 phone calls asking for verbal information."

"It's hard to keep information available far enough in advance," Rapalee finds. "Magazines work way ahead. It's tough getting information and photos from the curators." Local newspapers send reporters, but the city's television stations do not. Occasionally, a foreign television crew arrives to cover a show lent by their country's museums. Rapalee feels that "with more staff, we might be able to generate media attention, though T.V. crews don't like to travel." While most museums rely on public service announcements for advertising, Rapalee is pleased that her employer bought both prime-time and fringe-time television spots, beginning in 1985. Underwritten by local corporations, an outside agency prepared the 30-second commercials, which include a five-second blurb at the end for each of six individual sponsors. Full-page newspaper ads, using text and visuals from the television spot, were paid for by a volunteer group responsible for major fund-raising activities and the corporate sponsors, all of whom were invited to contribute again for 1986 commercials.

The public relations director is expected to attend evening openings, but Rapalee's hours are generally 9 A.M. to 5 P.M. "Salaries in museums are low, but benefits good," she comments. "Sometimes I feel I'm captive here because they make it so sweet. I can walk to work. Because I'm an artist, I'm in an environment I like to begin with. Leaving at 5, I'm home at 5:30, and can be in the studio by 6:30. Painting helps me unwind." She also praises the four-week vacations and excellent medical and dental benefits.

While in graduate school for her master's in fine arts, Rapalee had miscellaneous part-time jobs and came to realize that an artistic environment was important to her. Answering a local weekly newspaper ad led to her museum job, where she gets a chance to use her knowledge of art, though she does not spend much time in the galleries themselves. Enjoying the setting, she finds, "it helps a lot to have an arts background." In her boss, the public relations director, the museum seeks someone "who eats, sleeps, and breathes art, especially contemporary, and knows art publications and critics well. Having contacts helps."

For Rapalee,

> Working in a museum has given me another sense of the art world. I studied art publications and learned the commercial side working in a gallery. Working in the director's office was

excellent basic training in the museum's style of operating. My museum contacts are very useful; I get advice from the staff, and curators spoke to my women artists' group. At least I know the score.

PUBLIC RELATIONS IN A COMMUNITY DEVELOPMENT ORGANIZATION

"I'm head of a division—and the only one in it," laughs Wendy Weller, public relations director of a 46-member community development organization. Serving a population of more than 100,000, the 11-year-old nonprofit organization runs programs in housing rehabilitation, commercial revitalization, youth employment, refugee services, crime prevention, apartment referral, and neighborhood promotion. Weller promotes and writes press releases for all of the organization's programs, sets up press conferences, and arranges ribbon cuttings. Her 9 A.M. to 5 P.M. job expands for many evening meetings with various volunteer groups. After seven years, she is finally getting a full-time assistant. "My job is neighborhood promotion and special events," she explains. Each year, she puts together a seven-block street fair including a 3.5-mile race for 400 runners, a Victorian house tour, and an event such as the organization's tenth anniversary gala, which included an outstanding historical advertising journal. For the quarterly newsletter, read by 10,000, Weller writes and edits many of the articles and sells all of the advertising. An outside editor shares the responsibilites. Weller is currently reworking the group's magazine, "a real promotional tool." She works with volunteers and graphic designers on their direct-mail pieces and supervises the premiums offered in the "friends" mailings.

A community resident, Weller "was always an activist. I was the first woman on the board of [a smaller neighborhood group], for whom I ran house tours. I was very active on the board of my kid's private school. My job is really a paid extension of volunteer work. Now it's harder to get volunteers." She heard about the opening through her community grapevine.

"My biggest job," Weller claims, "is trying to change people's perceptions of this community. Houses sell for up to $400,000 but the media are negative. Interesting people are moving to the area now—artists, writers." The best part of her job is "working with community people, seeing changes that show the organization I'm part of has literally saved the neighborhood. To work and play in the same place is really very nice." However, Weller sometimes find working and playing in the same place to be a drawback. She notes that she has frequent fantasies of "going to work downtown." She also finds the public's perception of the neighborhood frustrating. "We know how good we are, but it's hard to get that message out. We never have enough money for anything," Weller says, echoing the standard nonprofit lament.

Weller, former theater major with some journalism background, says, "What I've brought to the organization is the ability to recruit people to work for their neighborhood. I got a local resident, an editor, to donate writing, editing, and photography for our revised magazine, a guide and map to the area." Spending most of her time in the office, Weller has to raise the funds for any events she creates, though she tries to have each one be a money-maker. She also solicits contributions from neighborhood businesses, such as when she persuaded the local gas company to print a poster promoting an activity. Weller prepares all year for the fall "Frolic," which attracts as many as 125,000 people for free entertainment on two stages, plus exhibit and merchandise booths and a footrace.

Weller also finds and supervises scores of volunteers to help on assorted projects. The organization has a before-and-after slide show of buildings it helped rehabilitate and other projects which have improved the area. Weller arranges to show it at hosted evenings for small groups of new homeowners, where "Friends" literature is distributed. She also places the organization's two major traveling exhibits, on Victorian homes and Art Deco apartment buildings, in banks or other public spots in the surrounding areas.

The most important traits for her work, Weller believes,

in addition to writing skills and flexibility, include "a good sense of humor. Be very outgoing. Work well with people, and love to be with them. Believe in what you're doing."

PUBLIC CONTACT IN A BOTANICAL GARDEN

Elvin McDonald has the ultimate public relations job: a position created especially for him. Now director of special projects for a famous botanical garden, McDonald was always "a gardening journalist." He has written 40 books, edited horticultural magazines, taught classes about plants, and done volunteer work at his local public garden. He joined the staff as a working gardener for half of 1985 to research a new book. "I didn't want to take notes in front of the gardeners, but occasionally I brought a camera. I loved the experience of working with 17 full-time gardeners, and about 17 aides and summer interns. I kept a diary on my train ride home for the book *Gardening with the Best*." Half the royalties will go to the gardeners. For two hours each day, he also worked on his syndicated twice-weekly column for King features.

McDonald was invited to become director of special projects because the organization "wanted a celebrity gardener." He serves as liaison to the city's cultural administration, providing plants and flowers for special events at city hall and for the department of parks and recreation. He makes arrangements for city events held at the garden and gives lectures in the suburbs and in other cities. McDonald was featured on a PBS special about the garden and is currently consulting with "20/20" on a gardening segment. He has appeared on Barbara Walters's and Phil Donahue's talk shows, among others. Like most nonprofits, the botanical garden is seeking publicity and more members. One of McDonald's ideas for generating publicity is an exhibit of gardeners' uniforms at the local museum; he will bring staff gardeners, modeling historic uniforms, on television talk shows when he is promoting his book. McDonald also writes articles for the garden's quarterly newsletter and *Plants and Gardens* handbooks, and will be producing educational videos.

"This is the happiest I've ever been," exclaims McDonald, who has gardened since age three. Although he was offered college scholarships in horticulture, McDonald accepted a larger grant from a music college and trained for a career in opera. His first job, however, was with *Flower and Garden* magazine in Kansas City. "After a work-a-holic phase, I took ten years off from books," the Oklahoma native reminisces. Eventually, he became senior editor at *House Beautiful*, and then published a successful independent newsletter before taking two years off to "travel everywhere and try to decide on a career move." He discovered he was "longing for the outdoors, and didn't want to do all writing/editing anymore. I didn't want to build my own large private garden, either." Friends encouraged him to join his hometown garden, to which McDonald has donated 40,000 horticultural slides. Now, claims McDonald, "I feel like a burden has been lifted. When I first came here, I thought I wanted to make a lot of money. Now I have this garden, where I can go out to welcome 600 people at the Azalea Ball, or simply the next 100 kids who get off the bus here."

McDonald thinks of it as "his" garden and believes that the entire staff shares this sense of personal involvement. He has always liked helping, entertaining, and motivating others. "I love the people here," he reports. Now working administrative hours, 9 A.M. to 4:30 P.M., he reads the paper on the train or enjoys a leisurely drive to work; his job includes a parking spot. The garden's staff of 200 includes almost as many security guards as gardeners, according to McDonald, who enjoys chatting about his work place. "Teachers here are paid less than gardeners and often leave to become gardeners," he explains. His organization boasts the first Children's Garden, built in 1914, which has served as a model for most others in this country and in Western Europe.

9

The Administrative Areas

INTRODUCTION

The people in personnel, accounting, finance, data processing, property management and maintenance, and all the clerical and secretarial functions are the ones who really keep a nonprofit organization moving on the day-to-day level.

These departments or positions exist in profit-making companies, too, and one might wonder what makes someone choose a nonprofit organization for an administrative career. Bill Olsen, former headmaster at a typical New England prep school, notes that the support staff of a nonprofit organization may have different motivations from those of nonadministrative employees.

> Clerical, maintenance, and dining hall employees do not carry out the specific mission of the organization. It's a *job*. They may stay because they like the ambience or the coworkers, and it's more pleasant than a farm or a factory. Our support staff were drawn mostly from [the] local population, and

we had to pay competitively with local businesses. The secretaries were well educated, thoughtful, and liked dealing with the professional staff. There was a lot of stimulation for the clerical staff, who served as a bridge between professional staff and background workers.

FUNCTIONS OF SECRETARIES/ ADMINISTRATIVE ASSISTANTS

Lorraine Smith, secretary at the University of Judaism "likes the camaraderie, the comfort of being in a Jewish atmosphere. In small schools, you know everyone. And you don't go through 42 people to get to someone. I like the student contact." Gwen Pemberton, personnel specialist at AFS International, a worldwide student exchange program, enjoys her job because "it's organic. AFS will never be like it was yesterday. You can learn and get your hands into so many pies. In personnel elsewhere, I feel I'd be more limited and reined in."

Pemberton's main responsibilities include recruiting and interviewing prospective employees. She tries to match candidates to the work style of the supervisor and interviews an average of three people a day. Most managers, she finds, "want free thinkers, independent workers with perfect skills." AFS conducts student and cultural exchange programs and has 61 offices around the world, with about 200 full-time employees in the United States headquarters office, and ten in Brussels. When hiring staff, she looks for "a sense of humor, interpersonal abilities, flexibility, initiative, good judgment, patience, creativity, problem solving, and the ability to deal with ambiguity. A lot of phone work is involved. AFS has a fast pace. Supervisors aren't always available, so employees need a sense of when to move and when to wait."

Administrative assistants at AFS are usually college students on their first jobs, often with liberal arts degrees. Entry salaries are $13,000 to $14,000. Because the job involves a great deal of paperwork, typing or word-processing skills are necessary. AFS will train employees in word processing. Pemberton seeks "promotable types" as administrative assistants because they are "image makers with heavy public contact. Often, they...return to graduate school or elect to pursue international affairs in another way. Others get promoted."

As in other fields, the secretarial/administrative assistant entry path can be highly effective. Coauthor Carol Milano, as a newly graduated English major, launched her career in 1967 with a secretarial spot on a U.S. Department of Labor grant at the National Student Association. The technical assistance project involved her in preparing a newsletter and training manuals, and serving as a clearinghouse for information used by local nonprofit agencies all over America. After five months, the project director unexpectedly resigned, leaving the secretary as the only full-time employee who knew the daily workings of the program. Assisted by more experienced, older officers of the association, Milano was groomed to take on more responsibilities, including planning and participating in regional training programs in the South, Southwest, and Pacific areas. By the time the grant ended in 1969, the former secretary was the acting project director, imbued with new, marketable skills in training, program design, and editorial work, plus, more importantly, self-confidence and a track record.

Not everyone wants to scramble up the pyramid, however. Lorraine Smith, a new grandmother and former New Yorker, says, "I'm comfortable. I like the environment. At this stage of life, I'm not too ambitious. Everything's slower in California; there's a different speed out here. It's less hectic than New York." Much of her work involves student records; she handles registration, grades, marking sheets, and transcripts for about 200 students in a cheerful office on a lovely campus atop Los Angeles's Mulholland Drive.

When Marcus Laster, executive director of Har Zion Temple, hires support staff, he looks for good interpersonal and public contact skills and telephone manner. For the top-level positions, it's important to be part of the congregation. For secretaries, bookkeepers, and receptionists, I'm not even sure they need to be Jewish! Keeping confidentiality...is important; people with problems come to see the rabbi, so you may hear pieces of their exchange. Respect for privacy is needed, and you must care about helping people.

Laster believes nonprofit organizations have to be competitive in the marketplace to keep competent administrative staff. "I pay my secretary what my mother, a real estate manager, pays hers," he explains.

FUNCTIONS OF UPPER-LEVEL ADMINISTRATORS

Administrative positions can involve taking on major responsibilities for the organization. As fiscal manager of the Alaska Repertory Theater, Alice Chebba handles their payroll, data processing, and all other computerized services. She prepares budgets, reports to the board and the finance committee, and supervises bookkeeping, the house manager, and concessions operations at the theater. She works on the annual audit and writes grant proposals for federal, state, and municipal funds, which bring in over $1 million a year. The company's annual budget is $3 million, and the full-time, year-round staff of 16 jumps to 200 when seasonal employees (artists, directors, and box-office personnel) are on hand. At the Alaska Repertory since May 1984, Chebba likes it very much. She has been involved in theater since high school and also earned a master's degree in public administration for nonprofit management. A vacation in Alaska stimulated her interest in living there, and she was hired over the telephone when the regional-theater grapevine carried news of her current job. "I absolutely feel an attachment to the company," she says. "I write the grants that raise the money to raise the curtain on the productions. I've learned a lot on the job, about myself, how I work with people, technical skills. I'm involved in policy decisions for my department, and consulted by the general manager."

Sensitive to fiscal matters, Chebba notes that "Alaska Rep pays quite well compared to other nonprofit theaters, though the cost of living is also very high. We get excellent benefits—medical, dental, and optical. Overtime work is paid. Our general manager insists on letting employees know they're important. The pension plan provides 3 percent of each employee's gross income annually." Her only complaint focuses on the location, not on her job. "We're isolated from the rest of the country. We spent $250,000 last year on transportation and housing, and we have to pay more to lure performers. We do one show in the summer and a regular season in winter, but *no one* wants to come to Alaska in the winter. It's hard and cold."

Chebba finds her career challenging, but admits, "I'd like to make more money and still enjoy my work if possible." While the income is quite adequate for her current needs, she concludes from observing friends, "it's hard to support a family on two nonprofit salaries."

Another relocation, albeit a less dramatic one, led to Julie Gillis's job as assistant director of national properties for the Girl Scouts of the United States of America. Gillis was a social worker for the state of Michigan for eight years. She was employed at a residential treatment center for adolescents, where her work involved some management of the property. In her spare time, she managed the housing development where she lived, and for three years she sold residential real estate, part time, until the market collapsed. Eventually concluding that Detroit offered limited opportunities, she decided to explore other possibilities, hoping to use her degree in Asian studies.

Because of her social-work background, a friend of a friend told her about the Girl Scouts, who regularly list jobs at their national headquarters, at their field offices in New York, Chicago, and Dallas, and at the 336 regional councils, each of which has an executive director, president, public relations specialist, and administrative staff.

Gillis's department oversees the national headquarters and the three field offices. Describing herself as "mainly a facilitator and budgeter," she works closely with the insurance and purchasing departments and is involved with space planning, renovations, and purchases. She makes budget decisions on maintenance, repair, and restoration; sees Girl Scouts when they visit headquarters; and deals with carpeting, furniture, and other vendors. After three years there, she comments:

> My values are consistent with those of the organization. The Girl Scouts combine many of my ideals: ecology, women's issues, youth development. I'm never asked to do anything immoral, underhanded, or unethical—building construction is fraught with bribes, but I just gasp "This is the Girl Scouts!" In nonprofit, you wear many hats, doing everything from getting light bulbs changed to buying and selling property. I like the chance to learn about office systems or museum record keeping. Every little bit of background has come into play in this job.

Besides the diversity, Gillis appreciates her recent promotion, and the fact that she is earning "a decent salary." (Professional salaries in her department range from $18,000 to $50,000.) Her hours are officially 8:30 A.M. to 4:30 P.M., but she generally stays until 5:30 P.M., as well as working evenings and weekends when work she supervises is going on. Says Gillis, "Carpeting is installed beyond office hours, so I'm there. What if the wrong color carpeting arrived?" Phone calls are constant during office hours, so Gillis stays late to write. "But I can take a two-hour lunch if I need to, because my boss is flexible," she points out.

The environment is pleasant, the facilities well maintained, and the coworkers nice. "We have a cafeteria in the building, and get tuition reimbursement, after one year, for job-related courses. I used to get six weeks vacation in Michigan and fabulous benefits; here I get four weeks vacation and good benefits. I'd consider a high-level job at a local council," she concludes, reflecting her continuing enthusiasm for the Girl Scouts and its work. Asked to cite the disadvantages of her job, Gillis says "like any corporation, we have unwieldy red tape, approval procedures, and committee decisions."

Many nonprofits, most often churches and universities, own and manage properties. Other nonprofits may receive sizable properties by bequest, or rent out part of the space in buildings the organization owns. If you have any experience in real estate, it can qualify you for a job in this specialty.

Property management jobs require the type of people skills that Julie Gillis's social-work experience provided, and call for both tact and writing ability. She says "I complain on paper to vendors, or send memos to the staff about building matters. I'm discovering more mechanical aptitude than I'd expected: I can understand heating and cooling and wiring." She coordinates the many parties and conferences held in the headquarters building and arranges the renovation of one or two floors each year, "which means disrupting everyone, organizing the vendors, and getting everyone back to work with as little havoc as possible." Gillis's involvement with the board includes "providing facilities for their meetings, contacting the caterers, and making all the arrangements. I come in at 7 A.M. when the board is in town." She also provides research materials for proposals her boss may be presenting.

The Girl Scouts own a diverse group of properties, including a ranch in Wyoming, which is used for outdoor education, horseback riding, and photography. Gillis inspects the property on horseback when she visits, because roads are limited. The historic home of founder Juliette Lowe, in Savannah, is being restored to its original Victorian condition and has a full-time curator on the premises. For the Savannah site, "museum-quality inventory procedures," another new area for Gillis to learn, are being designed. A marketing office in Randolph, New Jersey, will be both the warehouse and the base for Girl Scouts merchandise sales representatives. The Girl Scouts have built a suburban conference center on donated land previously used as a camp and leader-training site. One of Gillis's first tasks was working out the kinks in the new center, such as drains that did not drain.

Gillis's office also supplies support as requested to the 336 local councils, which are supported by sales of the famous cookies. The national office operates on dues paid by the 3 million Girl Scouts and the profits from merchandising. Gillis's office oversees the national headquarters and the field offices. "As a nonprofit agency, we get government surplus, which I distribute. This includes Department of Defense leftovers, like the piano from an officers club, or vehicles, parachutes, and typewriters. I approve requests from the regional councils, untangle the paperwork and red tape."

Gillis appreciates the value the Girl Scouts places on a volunteer's background. Executive Director Frances Hesselbein, in fact, is a former volunteer. "It's a woman-dominated environment," Gillis comments. "Men do work in data processing, audiovisual, and mail departments, but many of the staff were Girl Scouts, and volunteers often do move to jobs at the local councils, or on to national-level positions."

Gwen Pemberton is aware of the predominance of women at her organization, too, and claims, "we're trying to get a better distribution of males and females." Like the Girl Scouts, AFS attracts former volunteers to work at the organization. Many employees are former AFS exchange students or hosts of high school club members. Pemberton frequently gets unsolicited resumes from former hosts or students. "I do lots of 'courtesy interviews,' because we have so many volunteers. I really will call back if a suitable opening occurs," she maintains. Staff referrals are a good source for new employees, and AFS uses employment agencies when faced with simultaneous openings.

Pemberton likes personnel because, "I work with so many different people: staff, volunteers. It's very much like working in theater, because you write a script, have the whole idea, but something may still overthrow your plan. You have to fix it, and move on." She has considered leaving, but never has. She was a field consultant and regional manager for AFS before shifting to the personnel department, and she has found AFS alumni miss the challenge when they leave.

"We have an opportunity for dialogue among all levels on the staff, in an informal but business-oriented hierarchy. You can bitch and moan here, and be heard. I don't miss the volunteer involvement, the management, or the travel [of my former position]." On the negative side, she allows, "I feel less powerful in personnel. The people I hire leave to work for someone else. I love the people contact, but I'm totally removed from program running."

EXAMPLE OF AN ADMINISTRATIVE ASSISTANT

A feeling of separation from the actual delivery of an organization's service is common among administrative personnel, but this does not necessarily mean that employees feel detached or uninvolved. Jackie Vance (her name has been changed at her request), administrative assistant to a large university's school of journalism, observes, "you get involved with your own school or department rather than the larger university community. The department is an entity unto itself, often separate—attitudinally and physically, perhaps in another building." Reporting directly to the department chairman, Vance supervises the secretarial staff and delegates tasks, doing no secretarial work herself. "I'm in charge of the department budget, including grants, fellowships and gifts. I do class schedules, all the adjuncts' paperwork, and keep the faculty happy." Functioning like an office manager, she supervises two full-time secretaries and several work-study students. Calling the job "refreshing," Vance likes "the coworkers, students, the people. Paperwork doesn't change; it's the environment that counts. You can get positive feedback for improving the conditions of faculty and students." By streamlining the work flow of her department, she claims "I no longer deal with aggravated personalities. Simplifying the faculty's job makes life easier and more rewarding for me."

Vance enrolled in a career change workshop in 1979, just after quitting her job as customer-service supervisor at a small, family-run supply company. By coincidence, a temporary employment agency soon sent her to fill an opening in an area studies department at the very university where she had just completed the workshop. Hired permanently as a secretary, she was promoted to administrative assistant within four years.

She shifted departments when a restructuring at the area studies program was soon to eliminate her job. "Administrative assistants are not covered by the union, and I got no support from the university personnel office to find a new spot," she complains. Her own vigorous efforts led to her current position, but she has "learned the limitations of university careers without a master's degree. The higher the job, the more specific the requirements. The university is very inflexible about requirements for a job." The free-tuition benefits plus awareness of promotions requirements ("they're hinged to possibly irrelevant paper credentials") encouraged her to enroll in their master's program in public administration, with a possible finance concentration.

Of her six-and-a-half years on campus, Vance says:

> I've been lucky. I set my own time as long as I put in 35 hours a week and get the work done. That can mean 8:30 to 4:30, or 10 to 6. My first department head was very flexible about days off. I've had a free hand at both departments, and a lot of autonomy. I don't feel any pressure. Working conditions can always be improved, but by and large, aren't bad. I have my own office, though some of our faculty double up.

She cites one major negative: "We're definitely underpaid. The generous vacation time doesn't help, because you can't go anywhere. Free tuition is nice, but I wouldn't call it money in the pocket. It's time to make some money now. I'm not 25 anymore." She is in no particular hurry to move on, but is keenly aware of her limited advancement opportunities without a graduate degree. Today, starting salaries for department secretaries at the university are about $14,000; many keep jobs while pursuing an undergraduate or graduate degree, and then leave for a better-paying position, creating consistent openings at the entry level.

As in other areas of nonprofit, administrative staff have

the same ample time-off provisions. University of Judaism's Lorraine Smith comments "an advantage here is getting both national holidays and Jewish holidays. Our vacations are two weeks the first and second year, three weeks in the third and fourth years, and four weeks thereafter."

SUMMARY

Jobs in operations, accounting, and data processing are similar to analogous positions in for-profit companies. Salaries also tend to be similar, though not equal to, corporate rates in the same location. It is worth exploring opportunities in the support areas of nonprofit if you would like your efforts to contribute toward a worthwhile goal, benefiting other people. If you have a personal attachment to a particular cause, such as conservation or an illness that affects a family member, you may well derive deep satisfaction from being part of an organization involved with the issue. An unusual or very attractive environment like a zoo, botanical garden, or rolling rural campus may be a big attraction, too—especially if you don't like the idea of working in a skyscraper or large impersonal business office.

10

Government: The Nation's Largest Employer

INTRODUCTION

While it may seem hard to believe, over 16 million Americans, or 16.5 percent of the total work force, are employed by federal, state, or local governments. While no book on careers in the nonprofit sector can omit this vast job area, it is so enormous and so distinctive that it really requires a book of its own. We would just like to provide brief guidelines on how and where to get information about government employment, and to give some notion of the range and characteristics of these jobs.

FEDERAL JOBS

On the federal level, everyone is familiar with the giant agencies, like the Internal Revenue Service (IRS), the Federal Bureau of Investigation (FBI), and the Army. Fewer people are aware of the fact that the government also offers a wide range of quite specialized positions. For example, Jonathan Ballou is a genealogist at the National Zoological Park, involved in computerized matchmaking for endangered species all over the world. Field workers for the Indian Health Service help members of reservations in the Western states cope with physical problems arising from changes in their life-styles. Bruce Leonard, a public health worker in Zuni, New Mexico, established track and exercise programs for the 25 percent of Zuni adults who have developed diabetes.

Many government positions have traditionally been male dominated. Today, however, this is changing. Five years ago, the Federal Drug Enforcement Agency had fewer than 50 female agents; 183 women now make up 8 percent of the force. Two of today's women agents are in overseas posts; a third, Joan Marin, hopes her 21-year-old son will follow her into a federal drug enforcement career, making them the first mother-son team in agency history. Most of the women work undercover, using ingenuity in place of brute strength. The agency is making an active effort to hire and promote women. Eight percent of the Foreign Service now consists of husband-wife teams, who are assigned together whenever possible. Problems can arise at midcareer, however, due to agency policy against spouses supervising each other. This sometimes leads to one spouse taking unpaid leave rather than living apart.

Federal opportunities fluctuate with budget cuts (or increases) and elections. In the Reagan years, budget-balancing goals have led government to trim staff and programs. However, exceptions always exist: for example, current shortages of entry- and senior-level applicants in electrical engineering and computer specialties are reported. The Central Intelligence Agency (CIA) has introduced more aggressive and visible recruiting methods, including more campus visits. The Office of Personnel Management is, in fact, eager to expand its college recruitment, and will rejuvenate its newsletter, *Trends in Federal Hiring*, targeting it toward college-placement offices.

Salary

Traditionally, the federal government has tried to keep salary levels close to those in the private sector, in order to retain top talent. (In engineering and computers, however, parity has been difficult to maintain; newer, more modern equipment in the business world also attracts new graduates.)

An informal survey of some local newspapers revealed the following government jobs and salaries: appraiser for a big-city housing agency, starting at about $27,000 with two years' experience; research analyst in operations for an urban fire department, requiring a master's degree and one or two years of related experience, at $27,000 to $32,000; director of real estate and development for a regional rapid transit district, requiring about five years' experience, offering a minimum of $4,840 a month; and research-evaluation-policy manager for a state agency, requiring a B.A. and four years' experience and paying $27,000 to $37,000. School systems are a gold mine of opportunity. One major city sought a chief of transportation to manage and operate a large school bus fleet, at a salary between $42,000 and $62,000. To negotiate for its 5,000 employees, another urban district needed a director of staff relations, who would be paid $40,000 to $52,000. The Board of Cooperative Education Services (BOCES) in an affluent suburban county needed a director of interscholastic athletics with three to five years of school administration background, at a salary of more than $50,000. Two other suburban school districts advertised for superintendents, at salaries between $70,000 and $80,000. Climbing the managerial ladder in public service can lead to great challenge and responsibility, at livable, if not lavish, salaries.

Advantages of Federal Jobs

What are the advantages of a job with the federal government? We asked Pamela Talkin, assistant director of the San Francisco region of the National Labor Relations Board, which protects workers and helps settle labor-management disputes. A former high school Spanish teacher, she started as a field examiner, investigating West Coast cases, 12 years ago. "I enforce a law I believe in," Talkin affirms. "I think it's important work. I have interesting coworkers, a lot of independence, and a chance to use my own judgment. The work is varied and constantly changing. I like it a lot." Describing hers as "a federal but independent agency, with under 3,000 employees," Talkin notes that the exam she took to get her first job is no longer required. Field examiners travel about 20 percent of the time, are out of the office a good deal, and generally spend one night a week away from home. Starting salaries are about $18,000, with good benefits. Employees contribute to both health and pension plans. Vacations are a generous four weeks after three years of service, with 13 sick days a year. Talkin feels fluency in Spanish helped her get a job in a heavily Hispanic area. Now that she hires other people, she looks for common sense and good judgment, a professional demeanor, and strong interpersonal skills for interviewing or question-and-answer sessions. A background in economics or industrial relations is useful, but experience is not required.

Contrary to what many people believe, government jobs are not all part of a big bureaucratic maze. Carolyn Angiolillo joined the Urban Park Rangers, part of her mid-Atlantic city's parks and recreation department, in 1979, because she had "always wanted to work outdoors. I didn't like skyscrapers, and I loved walking around, being in the park, not having to get dressed for work, and, expecially, all the environmental stuff—like teaching kids about weather." She found the job through a professor at her college, who let her know when the rangers were just beginning. She had been seeking a post with the National Parks Service but had found it too competitive. Today, rangers start at $10.64 an hour, or about $19,000 a year. The city recruits every November and December for seasonal jobs, beginning in May and ending on Labor Day. At 500 to 600 colleges, they work through the placement office in the physical education or recreation and environmental studies departments, in addition to sending representatives for Career Days. Some 60 rangers are hired each summer. "If you want to stay on, and have done well, usually you can, due to the high turnover," Angiolillo explains. "People return to school, get promoted, or leave for other jobs."

In her years with the rangers, Angiolillo moved up to become deputy director and then acting director. She describes her job as "very creative. . . . Whatever you think of can be done. When I had a Mandarin-speaking ranger, we set up park tours in Chinese. Any talent can be utilized. No matter how consistent the job was, it changed whenever new staff arrived." As deputy director, she managed seven supervisors in charge of up to 120 rangers. She visited different sites, and even in the off-season had at least 30 people reporting to her, at an office in the largest park. She also worked on a federal grant the rangers received, to expand services into poorer communities.

Administrative as well as nonsummer hours are 9 A.M. to 5 P.M.. The rangers work assorted shifts during the summer season: 9 A.M. to 5 P.M., noon to 8 P.M., or 4 P.M. to midnight when evening concerts are held in city parks. For parades, a 6 A.M. to 2 P.M. shift is scheduled. Supervisors also work the more unusual shifts, when needed.

What does it take to be a satisfied urban park ranger? According to Angiolillo,

> You must like people. People contact is continuous. When not giving programs in environmental education to all age groups, rangers patrol, give information or directions, and offer first aid. They have to be even keeled, friendly, and personable, since they're in uniform, representing the city, and serve as the eyes and ears of the parks. They act as a crime deterrent and see all classes of people. Rangers like the outdoors, nature, and the environment, and are generally young and energetic. A teaching background is common. Many rangers are avid health-food eaters or vegetarians. And they're not in a fast-paced atmosphere!

Angiolillo helped Boston and Buffalo launch similar programs, and reports interest from other urban areas. "It's such a cost-effective program" she points out. "Rangers perform many functions in one package. Responsibilities are flexible, and a city gets a lot out of them." Look for comparable programs to be starting in other cities.

FINDING A JOB IN GOVERNMENT

Many government agencies are responsible for enforcing laws and thus employ huge numbers of attorneys. Prosecuting attorneys are the largest single group of state and local lawyers in government. Among lawyers for the federal government, 58 percent work in Washington, D.C. A monthly newsletter, *National and Federal Legal Employment Reporter*, describes jobs available. *Now Hiring: Government Jobs for Lawyers* is an American Bar Association manual that lists job descriptions, anticipated openings, locations, qualifications, and other information. The legal field offers a clear example of the salary disparities at different government levels. The starting salaries for 1983 law school graduates, as public defenders, were $11,000 to $24,000 (federal); $15,000 to $29,000 (state); and $13,000 to $25,000 (local). As prosecutors, 1983 graduates began at $20,000 to $25,000 (federal); $15,000 to $30,000 (state); and $15,000 to $28,000 (local).

How do you find out about government jobs? For current information about federal positions, check first in your telephone directory for the U.S. Office of Personnel Management; the nearest of fifty Federal Job Information Centers should be listed. These information centers provide general information about government jobs, guidelines on how to apply, and necessary application forms. They administer the written tests required for some titles. They will also help you determine which federal occupation matches your qualifications and let you know what positions you can apply for in the immediate location. Each state's department of civil service (or variation on that title) has an office in the capital, and one or more offices in other cities within its borders, offering free information about state jobs. Cities and counties have personnel offices, generally located near the executive office, dispensing information about jobs.

Government: The Nation's Largest Employer

About 3 million civilians now work for the executive branch of the government, and only 12 percent of them are in Washington, D.C. It is thus clear that federal jobs can be found all over the country. A biweekly newsletter, *Federal Career Opportunities*, is available from Federal Research Service, Inc., P.O. Box 1059, Vienna, Va. 22180. Their telephone number is (703) 281-0200. The newsletter costs $146 a year, and has many listings and very small print. It gives telephone numbers for the numerous federal agencies providing details on job openings by recorded phone announcements.

Federal Jobs Digest, a biweekly tabloid, is available from P.O. Box 594, Millwood, N.Y. 10546; it costs $29 for three months, or $110 a year. Each issue lists up to 16,000 jobs and includes handy articles on government job seeking. The *Digest* also publishes regional announcements and offers a matching service for subscribers, at a reduced fee, to help identify titles for which they may qualify. (No openings are guaranteed.) It covers jobs with salaries from $12,800 to $72,000. The toll-free number is 1-800-824-5000.

To get a federal job, you must follow the instructions in the announcement. Send an application to the Office of Personnel Management (OPM); if necessary, take a test. The OPM evaluates your qualifications and places your application in a competitive inventory. When openings occur, the federal agency requests a list from OPM's inventory; the best candidates are referred. The agency interviews candidates and makes their selection; civil service regulations require the agency to choose from among the three best applicants for each opening. State and local governments generally use a similar process.

At federal, state, city, and county agencies, many jobs, especially at entry level, are part of a civil service system, which contains some unique features. Intended originally to guarantee fair, unbiased selection of the best-suited candidates for a job, the system is also restricted by its own provisions. When test scores are the source of a new list of eligibles, direct experience or competence do not weigh as heavily as exam answers. Test scores are adjusted by the addition of "points" from other factors, typically military service, which adds a "veteran's bonus" to a test score. Some systems do give a set range of extra points for specialized experience or training. Hiring officials do have to proceed down the list, selecting among the top applicants; when eligible individuals decline job offers, names farther down the list will be considered.

The situation is neither bleak nor impenetrable, however; some positions, including nurses at municipal hospitals, are almost always open. Government jobs can be the best training ground for more highly paid positions. Middle- and high-level officials often shuttle between academia, government, and private industry, and often get involved in consulting work. Good access to media means that a capable public official can readily acquire recognition and visibility, both of which are helpful for whatever goal he or she intends to pursue.

The federal government is a major employer for lawyers, legislators, and engineers, and virtually the only job source for air traffic controllers and national law enforcement officers. At present, over 100 different agencies are operating; reorganizations occur frequently, so the exact number changes. Generally speaking, large agencies provide more jobs than smaller ones.

EXAMPLES OF JOBS IN FEDERAL AGENCIES

The U.S. Post Office is the largest and most ubiquitous employer, with 670,000 workers. To become a postmaster, experience in mail handling and distribution is required, so these managers come up through the ranks. The post office is the only federal agency with strong labor unions. Check with your local post office for news about employment tests for entry jobs (such as clerk or mail carrier).

The Social Security system has more than 33,000 representatives, administrators, and claims examiners in its offices all over the country. Nursing is another large employment area in the federal government; more than 35,000 R.N.s work at Veterans Administration (V.A.) sites, military units, public health service facilities, and clinics. The Federal Bureau of Investigation employs some 8,000 agents. The federal government operates some school systems, too, and has 14,500 teachers assigned to its Department of Defense schools for military families stationed overseas, and to the Bureau of Indian Affairs schools on Indian reservations. Nearly 10,000 physicians, mostly at V.A. hospitals, are with the federal service. More than 6,000 trainers instruct adults in crafts, trades, and professional skills, mostly in the army and air force; experience in the trade they train is needed. The military branches also employ the majority of 13,000 quality assurance specialists, who check on the goods produced at manufacturers' plants to fill government orders.

Procurement specialists, the government's purchasing managers, also negotiate and administer contracts. Over 90,000 engineers, in all the disciplines (aerospace, civil, electronic, electrical, and mechanical) work for the federal agencies. So do 17,000 lawyers. Professions within the federal system are as diverse as in the private sector. Technical and scientific positions abound, in accounting, auditing, computers, physics, chemistry, and forestry. Personnel administrators and management specialists are needed to take care of the employees of this huge system, and contact representatives advise the public about government programs, such as Social Security.

The executive branch of the government is the biggest employment area, though not the only one. The congressional division has 38,000 employees, and includes the General Accounting Office, General Printing Office, Library of Congress, and legislators. The staff for senators and representatives work on Capitol Hill as administrative assistants, legislative assistants, or case aides. Check with your state's senators and congressional representatives about the jobs available in their offices. In these jobs, one has to remember that your boss could lose the next election!

The General Accounting Office (G.A.O.) helps Congress watch over all the executive agencies. Its nearly 5,000 employees include accountants, auditors, economists, engineers, statisticians, computer specialists, and attorneys who help settle claims against the government. The G.A.O. announces current opening on a recording, at (202) 275-6017.

The General Printing Office publishes *The Congressional Record* and the *Federal Register*, and employs 9,000 people, mostly in the printing trades. The Library of Congress owns over 15 million books and 45 million other items. They provide information and research material to members of Congress, administer the nation's copyright law, offer reference services to the general public, and run scores of regional libraries for the blind or handicapped. Of the 4,600 employees, many have the master of library science degree. News about applying for jobs is available at (202) 287-5100.

The judicial branch, including the Supreme Court and the lower or specialized courts, employs about 15,000 people all over the country. The professional positions are judge, law clerk, bailiff, and guard; they work in district or appeals court, tax court, customs court, or the court of claims. Employment information is available only from the particular court in which you are interested. Check under the heading U.S. Government in the local telephone book.

An interesting example of a government agency is the Foreign Service, performing activities which go back as far as Ben Franklin's day. Its 7,000 officers and specialists include teachers, diplomats, librarians, translators, doctors, and nurses. Representing the United States 24 hours a day, these employees serve in 230 embassies and consulates. Because workers serve where the Foreign Service assigns them, regular moves are part of the job.

Consulates look after Americans in foreign countries and help out in case of emergencies or mundane problems. They issue visas to foreigners wishing to enter the United States. Economics offices are involved in international trade, the economic side of foreign policy, international investments, industrial development in other countries, and foreign exchange issues. Analysts track changes and trends in political climates overseas, and help negotiate agreements between American and foreign governments. Information officers function as the public relations department, representing America's policies and activities in other countries and maintaining our image by insuring clarity and understanding abroad. They also help arrange cultural exchanges between the United States and other countries. The Voice of American, broadcasting in 38 languages, is also part of the Foreign Service.

What traits does the Foreign Service seek in its employees? Tact and diplomacy, adaptability, exceptional interpersonal skills, intercultural awareness, communication, and persuasiveness on paper and in speaking are all important. Being well informed about politics is essential to these jobs, and a flair for languages is an asset. In fact, skills in languages like Russian or Chinese (increasingly needed in our international dealings) will mean a higher salary. The Foreign Service provides annual increases; salaries vary widely with job responsibilities. To qualify for a job, you must take the written exam given once a year; apply at the nearest regional Office of Personnel Management. The Department of State has an internship program for college students, with most of its positions located in Washington, D.C.

There is no central coordination of hiring for federal jobs, and you pretty much have to seek your own position. Some government jobs pay better than others; for example, salaries are not lavish for doctors, but they are excellent for beginning writers, compared to private sector earnings. The 1984 starting salary for college graduates was close to $14,000. Any government personnel office can supply current information on the rates for different grades of responsibility.

Here are some tips to help you in your federal job hunt. When filling out forms, it is imperative to answer every question fully. You can be disqualified for a slight omission, so be very careful and check your application thoroughly. The regional office of a government agency is likely to reply more quickly than the national headquarters when you request information. Often, a state employment service will keep federal job news and applications on hand.

STATE, LOCAL, AND ADMINISTRATIVE JOBS

The state government is an employment sector of its own, as a matter of fact. Each state is a service provider, with the biggest employment bases in hospitals, highway work, corrections departments, and welfare units. More than 13 million Americans work for state, local, and municipal governments, and with a turnover rate of 10 percent, that means an annual pool of 1 million jobs! These are true public service positions, comprising teachers, librarians, social workers, nurses, urban planners, college professors, fire fighters, judges, health inspectors, principals, building inspectors, sheriffs, gardeners, and many other titles. Salaries vary with location and position; some local governments are simply more solvent than others. This is a hard area to summarize, since it contains 80,000 separate employers: counties, municipalities, states, townships, school districts, and specialty agencies like authorities, boards, or commissions. Because politicians may control the budget and make the final decisions for some local agencies or positions, investigate job possibilities carefully. Will you need to be elected, appointed, or hired for a position? Is the job a civil service title? Residency is often a requirement for state or local positions, and it is almost always an advantage. U.S. citizenship is often necessary.

Local and state agencies usually make announcements of their openings. Start by checking at the main branch of the public library or the nearest state job service. Look in local newspapers, community organizations that offer employment information, or the college placement offices in your area. Professional associations in the field you are considering often know about government openings, so contact the nearest chapter. (You may have to start with the national office of a professional group to track down the branch closest to you; see Appendix A for a listing of these associations.)

Paid positions with local elected officials are a unique, interesting opportunity area. Salaries are paid out of a budget allocated for staff and services to each officeholder; while salaries can be very low, the jobs themselves offer a chance to take on a variety of tasks, acquire visibility and contacts in the local political arena, and develop sophisticated skills. Staff at local politicians' offices deal with current issues, solve constituents' problems, attend meetings, write press releases and deal with the media, work on fund raising, and represent the elected officer at community organizations and events. Particularly for those contemplating a career in politics or government, these jobs are excellent starting spots.

Why choose a career in government? While achievement can be hard to measure in many of the jobs mentioned in this chapter, the rewards are very significant: you make a real contribution to society, and, particularly in the federal system, earn a decent living with job security, excellent benefits, and fine opportunities for advancement. At state and local levels, you have a chance to make a perceptible impact on the community around you.

11

Targeting, Exploring, and Getting a Job

EXAMINING YOURSELF

If, after reading this far, you feel that a career in the nonprofit world might be right for you, the next step is strategic planning. To design an effective "marketing campaign," it is imperative to first know the "product": in this case, *you*. Take a long, honest look at your skills, interests, values, and temperament. What are you looking for in terms of hours, work environment, level of commitment, and salary? Are you willing to travel (or relocate) for a job? Would you rather work in a large office or a smaller one? Are you seeking a lot of autonomy, or do you prefer a structured set of responsibilities?

If you wish to pursue a career in nonprofits, you need to identify the causes or issues for which you feel passion, or at least admiration. To be successful, you must respect the purpose of the organization for which you will be working, and take pride in being a part of its efforts. Which organizations have you contributed to in the past? Are you a member of any nonprofit group? Which topics in the daily newspaper or newscasts evoke strong emotional responses? Did you join any committees in your community, college, or church? What do you do in your spare time? Are you involved in outdoor activities, a devoted performing arts fan, or deeply concerned with health issues? Which magazines do you subscribe to? The answers to these queries can provide valuable clues as to which causes you would be most happily involved in as a full-time employee. This will help you narrow the nonprofit universe down to the components that fit you best.

Most people are modest about declaring the things they are very good at. Learning to speak confidently and comfortably about your abilities is a necessary part of the job-hunting process, but it is one that evolves gradually. Here are two ways to gain a fairly objective view of your talents:

1. Make a list of all the accomplishments—academic, professional, personal, social, or avocational—that you take pride in. What do they show about your abilities? Does a pattern emerge, reflecting the abilities you use most frequently?
2. Ask three or four people who know you well—coworkers, friends, classmates, relatives—what they see as your most outstanding qualities. Often, we take for granted the things we do well, so it takes an outsider to point out real strengths.

Having established what you are able to do competently, take a look at your preferences. What do you wish you could be paid to do all day? Try to think of as many different activities as you can that you would find appealing. Eliminating the pipe-dream items, such as three-hour expense-account lunches, how many items on your mental or paper list have been mentioned as parts of various nonprofit positions? Do they cluster in one particular chapter? If so, you already have a tentative goal for launching your search. What if you are a generalist, with wide-ranging interests and many capabilities? This opens the largest number of possibilities, enabling you to look at an assortment of jobs in any agencies whose missions match your values.

If you are not interested in moving, consider geographic concerns early in your planning. What kinds of nonprofits are in commuting range of your home? Libraries, schools, and hospitals are accessible to most communities; other types of organizations simply may not operate in your area. For those in large cities, or those willing to relocate, the options are broad.

Are you willing to go back to school, if necessary? For most nonprofit positions, a specific graduate degree is not required, but you may improve your chances with carefully selected noncredit courses. Lacking an undergraduate degree will probably be a big disadvantage, so you may want to think about completing one.

RESEARCH THE FIELD
Printed Sources

After completing the "know thyself" phase, you need to start "reality testing." We have given you an overview of the nonprofit world to help you determine if you are interested enough to want to know more about a particular sector. For further research, go to the nearest career or business library. (CATALYST, a national nonprofit research group, compiles a list of career libraries. You can contact them at (212) 777-8900 or write to 250 Park Avenue South, New York, N.Y. 10016.) Whole books and directories are devoted to careers in health, medical services, education or social services, the arts, and government. Almost any library stocks the U.S. Department of Labor's *Occupational Outlook Handbook*, with its reliable quarterly updates. This is a good starting point, since it provides names of associations to contact for more information and gives the Bureau of Labor Statistics' predictions for employment opportunities in each occupation it discusses.

Study the trade publications in each specialty area that

interests you. Hundreds of magazines and newspapers serve the nonprofit world, including *Museum News*, the *Chronicle of Higher Education*, and *Fund Raising Management*. Many carry job listings, so you can gain a sense of where the needs and demands are, and what nonprofits are paying in different parts of the country. Read the trade publications carefully, first to see whether the issues in this field matter to you. If you are bored with all the topics covered in the monthly publication serving a specialty, you will not find them any more important when they are your full-time concern. You will also absorb the jargon of a field by reading its literature, and it is important on job interviews to be able to fluently speak the language of the interviewer.

Try to verify and expand your existing information during the research process. What kind of training seems most desirable to employers? Which employers earn the most positive notice? Is there a particular city or region where opportunities appear especially promising? Are there "movers and shakers" in this field, whose names crop up regularly? Which professional groups have the highest visibility? Pay careful attention to the help-wanted ads in the trade publications, for a current look at salaries in different parts of the country and an indication of the most valuable sorts of experience. You may not be ready for the highest-level jobs advertised, but ask yourself if this is the direction you would like to pursue. Avoid putting yourself into a dead-end situation as a career-changer; try to make sure the path you are considering has alternative forks.

Take systematic notes during your research. Keep track of the organizations with impressive programs or high earnings. Who are the prominent, most-quoted officials in a specialty, and where do they work? Note names and titles (and phone numbers); jot down a few words to help you remember what impressed you about this individual or agency. Set up a file folder or a box of index cards, so you can organize your jottings.

Continue the library research until you reach a significant plateau—the point when you are conversant in the jargon of the field, and the issues you read about are beginning to seem familiar. In other words, stay in the library until you can ask intelligent questions about the specialty you are exploring.

Professional Organizations

Contact the nearest professional association you have read about. Sometimes you may end up calling the national headquarters, but many groups have local chapters in each metropolitan area. Ask for any literature or publications they produce, and find out when and where their meetings are. Ask whether prospective members may attend and what the cost is. In some groups, nonmembers are discouraged, but you can be invited as the guest of a member. Occasionally, the person you are talking to can arrange for you to have a guest pass. If there is someone at the association's office who can talk with beginners in the field, ask if you can see that individual.

If at all possible, go to meetings of the professional organizations in the area you are exploring. You will be surrounded by practitioners in the field, and it is important for you to see who your future colleagues will be. Do you feel comfortable among this group? Do you look and sound like they do? Are these the sort of people you want to be around 40 or more hours a week for the foreseeable future?

While attending meetings of professional groups is an investment of both time and money, it can be invaluable if you maximize the opportunity. The best meetings are those with some sort of "mingle time" scheduled—usually a cocktail hour before dinner or lunch. This increases your chances to smile at and shake hands with the largest number of people, and when you are seated for the meal, you will automatically have a chance to meet everyone at your table. Far less effective is the presentation-only meeting, in which members arrive, are seated in a lecture hall or auditorium, listen to a talk by a distinguished colleague, and leave. You may be stimulated and informed by what you have heard, but the odds are slim that you will meet anyone personally when you are all seated in a big room listening to someone else.

NETWORKING AND INFORMATIONAL INTERVIEWING

Indeed, professional associations are often the first step in the much ballyhooed networking process. *Networking* is a straightforward, highly individual, purposeful approach to meeting and keeping in touch with an ever-expanding set of people whose interests intersect with yours in some way. Always remember, the object of networking is mutual benefit. It may be difficult as a newcomer to a field to see how it could possibly be valuable to an experienced professional to spend time helping you. The immediate benefit may be as intangible as doing a favor for an old friend, or as evident as helping a colleague find the perfect candidate for a new opening. This proven, established approach is based on the long-standing, extremely effective "old boys' network," and you can be assured that, under appropriate circumstances, people will assist you, too.

A good basic tool in your networking kit will be the directory of whichever professional group(s) you join. This will give you access to the hundreds or thousands of members who work in the field you have decided you would like to enter. We would like to spare you the experience referred to as the "cold calls," in which you telephone a total stranger who does not expect to hear from you to ask that person to do something. Cold calls are demanding and incur a high rate of rejection. We recommend you try "lukewarm calls," by first contacting people you met face-to-face, however briefly, at an association meeting. Your goal for the next phase is to meet with some experienced professionals in the field, so you can get the most current, realistic information of all. What you are trying to do now is set up a few *informational visits*, in which you will do your final "reality testing" to determine whether this specialty still seems right for you. One of the most important concerns is the work environment itself, so you need to visit people in their occupational habitat to get a real sense of what it is like, and whether it is compatible with your needs, values, and modus operandi.

We must warn you not to confuse this informational visit with a job interview. This is still part of your personal quest for information and validation. It would be premature for you to accept a job offer until you have had time to survey the work place, atmosphere, equipment, and other occupational features. You owe it to your own career planning to maintain an open mind and delay your decision making until you have conducted at least three on-site visits to the types of organizations for which you are contemplating working.

When you call someone you sat next to at a professional organization's luncheon meeting, identify yourself as briefly and quickly as possible. "Hi, this is John Smith. We had lunch together at the NAHD meeting last month." Always remember that you are interrupting when you call someone at work, so be courteous enough to ask if he or she has a spare moment. If the person does, continue by explaining your purpose. "I've been seriously exploring the possibility of a career (change) in (to) fund raising (or public relations or social work), and I've done a lot of reading in books and journals. Now I'm at the point where I need to speak to an experienced professional to find out if my research has been accurate and up-to-date. I've read a great deal about the outstanding work your agency has done, and I'd like to come by for about 15 minutes to ask you a few questions about what it takes to succeed in this field." (No informational visit since the dawn of humanity ever took 15 minutes, but you cannot ask a busy professional for an hour. Similarly, you should not tell them you are looking for a job, as that makes it too easy for a near-stranger to quickly dismiss you with, "Sorry, we have no openings right now." As we mentioned previously, you need to believe you are *not* looking for a job yet, but rather completing your thorough investigation of a prospective field.)

When you ask a responsible professional to take time to meet with you, be prepared to schedule the meeting at his or her convenience, not your own. If you are currently a full-time employee in another field, or a student, you will have to modify your own commitments to fit around your source's schedule. The quietest time of the day for him or her may be very early or late in the workday, when coworkers are scarce and telephones calm. Be as accommodating as possible, and don't make the other person struggle to find a 15-minute spot you can accept. Your tone should be cordial and appreciative, without being gushy or servile. It helps to remember that you cannot force anyone to say yes, so prepare yourself to hear a few responses like "This is the worst time of year for me; our budget is due and I won't have a free minute for three months." However, when people say they are happy to help, they probably are. It is very flattering to be regarded as an expert and to have an eager, alert beginner turning to you for advice and guidance.

On your informational visits, have a set of questions for which you would like answers. It is okay to jot down a note or two during the conversation. You will want to find out about the type of experience or training that serves a newcomer best, the responsibilities one gets at the beginning of a career in this field, the best organizations to work for, starting salaries, and possible career paths. What are the problems in this specialty? Is it expanding or shrinking? Try to weave in things you have learned during that stint in the library. Ask questions about new techniques or equipment you may have read about. Mention some key issues in the field to find out how they affect the professional staff. The person you are visiting should be impressed with how well prepared, serious, and thorough you are.

Do not overstay your welcome. Be sensitive to ringing phones or knocks on the office door. When you feel you have collected enough information, thank the person for the time he or she has given you. If it seems that rapport has been good, you can say before leaving something like "after talking to you, I'm even more excited about the possibility of this career move. Do you know anyone in a similar position at a much larger (or much smaller) agency who I could talk to to get another well-informed point of view?" Often, another name or two will be forthcoming, and you will then be able to call this new link in your network.

After an informational visit, always send a gracious thank-you note. It is important to keep doors open, so before you leave, ask if you can keep in touch. If you meet with someone recommended by your first source, call to describe the results of the second meeting and to say thank you. On each informational visit, be sure to pay careful attention to the atmosphere in the work place. How do the staff look—calm and happy or furrowed and frazzled? Are phones jangling and people yelling, or is the office humming efficiently? Is equipment old and archaic? Are employees crowded together? Do you see any windows? Every organization is different, but if you visit a few offices, you can begin to make some generalizations.

When you telephone a new source for your network, you can say, "This is John Smith, and Dave Clark at Municipal Hospital suggested I call you because I've been seriously exploring the possibility. . ." Your chances for an affirmative response are enhanced when you mention a mutual acquaintance, because your credibility is established with a stranger who thinks well of the person referring you. The only catch in these circumstances is that the new link may say, "Sure, I'll be glad to see you. Let's have lunch (dinner) (a drink) (coffee)." An important part of your mission is to see the work place, and that will not happen in a restaurant. Try to demur, as graciously as possible, by explaining why it is important for you to visit the agency itself. Your source may insist that it is too hectic in the office, with people barging in all the time, and that it would be awkward to talk. Under those conditions, accept a lunch or cocktail date (which you should expect to pay for), but explain that you would very much like to come by the office first, for a brief glimpse of the professional setting.

The other source for networking is, for want of a better term, everyone you've ever met: friends; family; coworkers; neighbors; members of your health club, block association, or religious organization; doctor; dentist; stockbroker; accountant; travel agent; lawyer, and so on. The more specifically you ask for assistance, the more likely you are to receive it. Formulate your request so that whoever you are asking understands clearly what you want. Again, you will need to reassure people that you are *not* looking for a job but are collecting expert information. "I've been seriously researching the possibility of a career in ____," you'll say to your uncle. "Now I'm at the point of needing to speak to people who really work in the field to find out if my information is up-to-date and accurate, in order to decide if I want to pursue this career. I'm not looking for a job yet, but this is the final phase of my research. Do you know anyone who works in a hospital?" If you truly ask everyone you know, and their parents or siblings, you are bound to come up with one or two leads. You may not find a person in the exact position you are exploring, but once you get to the purchasing agent or floor nurse in a hospital, he or she can steer you toward the head of the social services department. Alumni associations can be particularly valuable, too; old school ties often evoke a positive response.

Again, you will doubtless run into the "let's-have-lunch" catch, which you can handle as previously suggested. This networking phase is a good time for you to talk to as many people as you can, before you are a full-fledged job hunter. It will benefit you throughout your career to know others in the industry; they can help you when you need an assistant or information about a technical matter, and you can help them if they have a promotion to offer you.

When you have grown fairly comfortable making informational visits, there is one cold call that can be very valuable. If there is an organization or individual who impressed you very much in your research, you can make a cold call to try arranging an interview. Some people prefer to send a note first. On phone or paper, begin, if at all possible, by congratulating the individual on a recent award, promotion, election to a key position, or an insightful, well-written article in one of the professional publications. Then, in your second paragraph, offer your, by now familiar, explanation of who you are and why it would be enormously helpful to you if you could meet with this expert (who has just been very flattered by your astute and kind words) for a few minutes.

Before you balk at the contrived, transparent, and self-serving features of this approach, stop and think about the realities. This is not Bruce Springsteen you are trying to get together with. The public relations coordinator of a small college does not get such a large volume of fan mail that she is jaded about it. The nonprofit world is a service provider, and most of its officials work in the background, so they receive little public acclaim. It is a genuine pleasure for people to hear how their words and thoughts affected the reader, and under these circumstances, many people may be delighted to meet you for a few minutes. Remember, too, although you don't want to take advantage of it, that nonprofit careers are helping professions, and employees in this sector tend to be caring people. Even if they are genuinely too busy to meet with you, ask if there is another member of the staff you might be able to talk with, as part of your research. This approach is usually effective, but do rehearse what you are going to say before you call. You want to sound reasonably sure of yourself and of your reasons for selecting this individual.

Even if you write a letter first, providing your standard background information, the last line of your note should be something like, "I'll be taking the liberty of calling you next week." *Never* put the responsibility on a total stranger to take the initiative of telephoning you, as that places you at the disadvantage of having to wait by the phone. In our view, since you will have to telephone next week anyway, you might consider using your letter as a working "script," and then just pick up the receiver and dial. It saves a week of time. If you feel it is more courteous to forward some written information first, that's up to you, but realize that you will still have to remind the person of who you are, the purpose of your call, and what you would like him or her to do.

While letter writing may slow your explorations down a

bit, there is one kind of writing we advocate vigorously: jotting notes before you make networking calls. Give yourself cues about exactly which points to make, in order of priority. You may be a little nervous at calling someone you have not met to ask for a brief meeting, and even if you have practiced with the cat a couple of times, you may forget one key phrase during the actual conversation. Put yourself in the right setting for your telephone calls, too. One brilliant networker we knew would come home from school each day and shed his jeans for a suit and tie so he could feel like the professionals he was calling each afternoon. Keep your calendar next to the phone so you can make appointments smoothly.

HUNTING FOR A JOB
Use Your Network

Eventually, you will be ready to make a career decision; if all your findings lead to the conclusion that the field you are exploring seems right for you, then you are ready to move to job hunting. First, call each member of your network, and let them know you have reached a decision and are now looking for your first job in the profession. If they hear of anything, would they please let you know? Should you hear a lot of encouragement, ask if you can send a copy of your resume along. (Speaking of resume, do not worry about preparing yours until your research has revealed what kinds of skills and experience in this field carry the most weight. Then you can tailor your resume to reflect as much of this kind of background as possible. Members of your network may even be willing to comment on a draft version of your resume for you, pointing out the strong and weak features.)

Ask members of your network if you can give them a ring every few weeks to see if they have heard any job news on the grapevine. Find out if they know any inside news about organizations that may be expanding soon (for example, with a new capital campaign or a large grant). Contact the professional associations, especially if they have a regular job-listing service; if they don't, find out if there is an informal mechanism.

Use Printed Job Ads

It is not the best advice in most professions, but nonprofit is an exception: a high percentage of jobs in this field are found through ads in newspapers or professional periodicals. Often, an inexpensive ad is the most cost-effective way for a tightly budgeted nonprofit to catch the attention of well-qualified people. Of course, an advantage of going through your own network is that it gives you fairly unique access to possible openings; when you answer a newspaper ad, you are one among hundreds, so it's easy to get screened out. Do not send just a resume. Be sure to include a customized cover letter, stressing your interest in this particular position and highlighting the skills, talents, and experiences in your background that make you valuable to this employer.

Newspaper ads often give merely a box number, which leaves you in an awkward position in terms of salutation. "Dear Sir or Madam" is the formal, all-purpose greeting to an unknown reader; if you are the friendly, casual sort, consider "Good Morning" or "Dear Box 114." "To Whom It May Concern" is inexcusably stiff. Pay attention to any clues in the ad. Michael Jones got the inside track on his job because the newspaper ad specified only a nonprofit station in a particular city. By figuring out which NPR station operated in that location, he identified the general manager and sent a personal note, instead of using the box number, as all the other respondents had. The manager, now Jones's boss, was impressed with his resourcefulness, and interviewed him.

When you know which agency is advertising, answer the ad, then turn to your own network. Does anybody know anyone at this organization? If so, it is always better for you to apply outside the crush of other respondents. Make a direct phone call, if you can. Should someone in your network offer to mention you to a friend at the advertising organization, be grateful—and also ask if you could call the friend later on.

Employment Agencies

If you can find an employment agency that seems to have several nonprofit clients, visit them, and go on any interviews they can generate for you. It is to your advantage to visit all the nonprofits you can in your job hunt. Talking with an employment counselor will give you an up-to-date sense of salaries and your own worth in the local market. For budgetary reasons, however, most nonprofits would rather not pay employment agency fees, so do not choose this method in lieu of replying to newspaper ads.

Visits and Volunteers

Have you identified one or more not-for-profits you would like to work for? Go visit them directly. Turn to the members of your network to see if anybody has an acquaintance at the nearby community college or historical society. Chat with staff on your visit. Do not start with the personnel department, because if they haven't heard of any immediate openings, they will try to keep you from bothering anyone. The person you want to meet is the one in charge of the area in which you would like to work. A good way for you to sample the nonprofit organization you are considering, and to meet some of its staff members, would be to do some volunteer work for them, perferably while you are a student or still employed elsewhere.

As a volunteer, you will get an inside glimpse of what the agency really does, and you can begin to determine how you feel about their goals and way of working. If you are a student, you might be able to set up an internship to gain both experience and insight in a nonprofit area. One former banker, contemplating a career change, accepted an internship offered at the university where she was taking a continuing education course in fund raising. She liked the work so much, and was quick enough to see its potential, that she convinced her supervisor to find a part-time budget line for her. Excited at the polish and acumen her banking experience had provided, her supervisor convinced *his* boss to allocate a small salary, and the former banker spent a year learning on the job and establishing her credentials in a new field, before moving on to a full-time opportunity.

Maryann Alfano, now with the International Center for the Disabled, built her career change from office management by a year of unpaid service, planning special events at a prestigious hospital. She lived off her savings for a year, which she describes as difficult but worth it. "I got the hospital to let me say I'd been an intern for a year. I was looking for a $30,000 job, and got $25,000 with a director title." As Maryann's experience proves, when you talk about your experience, there is no need to label it paid or unpaid. What an employer cares about is that you have done the work described. Do not call yourself a "volunteer" in your resume or interviews. Simply describe the tasks you carried out, and how they benefited the organization.

INTERVIEWING

Job hunting is a two-way street. The interviewer is trying to find the best candidate for the job:; the applicant is looking for a satisfying position. The first thing you want to investigate is the organization itself, before you consider working there. Turn first to the members of your network, to get a reading on the reputation the organization has in the local nonprofit community. Try to get a copy of the latest annual report to read beforehand. If it is an organization that operates all over the country, the National Charitable Information Bureau (NCIB) keeps track of it and can send you a current report at no charge, if you request it in writing. (The NCIB address is 149 Park Avenue South, New York, N.Y. 10016.) The NCIB evaluates some 300 organizations in terms of how well they meet what are termed "the basic standards in philanthropy." If you have an appointment at a particular agency, ask if they can send you a brochure to read before your interview. The better informed you are before the interview, the sharper your questions will be. Interviewers are impressed with well-prepared applicants; this shows you are serious, hardworking, resourceful, and eager. People who do their homework when they do not even have the job will obviously be dedicated employees.

We all think of job interviews as a time when tough questions are thrown at us. Bear in mind that you may want to ask some questions too, because you will be making a decision at least as important as the agency. Lynne Hayden, who shifted into nonprofit from advertising sales, suggests some especially valuable questions for applicants to pose:

- How long have you been working here?
- Who will evaluate my performance on this job? What are the criteria?
- How big is the budget for the department I would work in?
- What is the support staff available to me?
- Who makes the final decision about this position?
- Where would I work? (If possible, you want to see the work site.)
- Who would I report to?
- Will the organization pay for membership in professional associations?

Following this chapter is a list of the questions Maryann Alfano asked during her career explorations. Many are good points to inquire about in actual job interviews, as well.

Before any interview, think through your replies to such predictable questions as, "Why do you want to work here?" "How does your experience relate to this position?" or "What do you know about this agency?" Anticipate questions about why you want to work in not-for-profit. If you are changing fields, it is likely that a starting salary may be less than your current earnings, which makes prospective employers nervous. They worry that you will be resentful and unhappy, and therefore will not do a good job for them. Reassure an interviewer about any reservations you realize they have. Try to dispel objections, even if they are not specifically stated. Sometimes interviewers use the catchall phrase "you're overqualified," to dismiss someone they are uneasy about for a range of possible reasons. Do not become defensive or unnerved if an interviewer murmurs "overqualified." Try to overcome the doubts underlying the phrase. You might respond as follows:

> I am well qualified for this position, certainly, and I have given my career path a lot of serious thought and research for the past several months. I am quite sure that I wish to be in this field now, and I fully understand that I may be paid less than I have been earning because that is the standard. I am financially able to maintain my current life-style with a somewhat reduced income, and I am eager to offer my abilities to your organization because I feel my level of satisfaction and professional pleasure will rise significantly. This is worth more than just dollars to me.

Every employer is looking for enthusiasm and cooperation in new staff members. Learn to frame your comments in terms of what you can do for the employer. Make it clear that your first concern is helping them do their work effectively, and that your skills and experience will be valuable to their purposes.

By the way, it is sometimes possible, once you are a leading contender for a job you know you want, to negotiate a bit on the stated salary. Both Fred Hart, moving from global banking to a hospital, and Lynne Hayden, leaving advertising sales for a community college, told their employers-to-be that they simply could not move for the offered salary because it was too dramatic a reduction in income. In both cases, the future boss came back with a somewhat better offer. (Hart, in fact, made a lateral move; Hayden earns half her previous salary.)

Do not feel that you must accept the first job offer you receive. It is important to look at the advancement potential and the health of the organization before you say yes. With systematic networking and job hunting, other offers will follow, so let yourself select wisely, rather than rapidly. Accepting a job is almost like getting married: you'll be spending a lot of time in this new role. Do you like the work setting? The people who will be your coworkers? Your future boss? Are you impressed with the aims and public perception of this organization? Are you excited about the tasks you will be doing in the new job? Do you care about the things that go on there? Can you live with the hours, salary, benefits, and working conditions?

If you can comfortably answer "yes" (or a very strong "I think so") to all of these crucial questions, go ahead and accept the position. And good luck in your new career!

QUESTIONS TO ASK IN AN INTERVIEW FOR A NONPROFIT POSITION

1. What do you do in a typical day?
2. What are your main job functions and duties?
3. What do you like and dislike about this job?
4. What unusual commitments does this job demand—such as overtime, travel, etc.?
5. What is the salary range for this job?
6. What is the chance to advance from this job? (Or: what are the various job steps that lead to this job?)
7. What special talents, training, or education are needed for this job?
8. What abilities and personal characteristics lead to success or failure in this job?
9. What are the future employment opportunities for this job—is this a growing field?
10. Does this organization have an affirmative action program to upgrade and promote women and minorities?
11. What percentage of managerial jobs are held by women in this firm?
12. What other opportunities exist in this field or industry for a person with my background and experience—or if I were to acquire the necessary experience and training?
13. Could you refer me to two other people in this company or industry whom I might interview for more information?

Associations

American Association for
  Counseling and Development
5999 Stevenson Avenue
Alexandria, Va. 22304

American Association for
  Respiration Therapy
1720 Regal Row
Dallas, Tex. 75235

American Association for State
  and Local History
1400 Eighth Avenue South
Nashville, Tenn. 37203

American Association of Museums
1055 Thomas Jefferson Street N.W.
Washington, D.C. 20007

American Association of
  University Professors
One Dupont Circle N.W., Suite 500
Washington, D.C. 20036

American Association of
  University Women
2401 Virginia Avenue N.W.
Washington, D.C. 20037

American College of Hospital
  Administrators
840 North Lake Shore Drive
Chicago, Ill. 60611

American Council for the Arts
570 Seventh Avenue
New York, N.Y. 10018

American Council of Learned
  Societies
228 East 45 Street
New York, N.Y. 10017

American Counseling Association
729 11th Avenue
Huntington, W.V. 25701

American Dietetic Association
430 North Michigan Avenue
Chicago, Ill. 60611

American Federation of Teachers
11 Dupont Circle N.W.
Washington, D.C. 20036

American Hospital Association
840 North Lake Shore Drive
Chicago, Ill. 60611

Associations 191

American Library Association
50 East Huron Street
Chicago, Ill. 60611

American Mental Health
 Counselors Association
CRAGS Building,
Pennsylvania State University
Middletown, Pa. 17057

American Nurses Association
2420 Pershing Road
Kansas City, Mo. 64108

American Occupational Therapy
 Association
1383 Piccard Drive, Suite 301
Rockville, Md. 20850

American Physical Therapy
 Association
1111 North Fairfax Street
Alexandria, Va. 22314

American Public Health
 Association
1015 15 Street N.W.
Washington, D.C. 20005

American Rehabilitation
 Counseling Association
2 Skyline Place,
5203 Leesburg Pike
Falls Church, Va. 22041

American Society of Personnel
 Administrators
606 North Washington Street
Alexandria, Va. 22314

American Symphony Orchestra
 League
633 E. Street N.W.
Washington, D.C. 20004

Association for Community-Based
 Education
1806 Vernon Street N.W.
Washington, D.C. 20009

Association for Hispanic Arts
200 East 87 Street
New York, N.Y. 10028

Association of Physicians'
 Assistant Programs
2341 Jefferson Davis Highway,
 #700
Arlington, Va. 22202

Association of Science-Tech
 Centers
1413 K Street N.W.
Washington, D.C. 20005

Center for Arts Information
1285 Avenue of the Americas
New York, N.Y. 10019

Center for Community Change
1000 Wisconsin Avenue N.W.
Washington, D.C. 20007

College and University Personnel
 Association
11 Dupont Circle N.W., #120
Washington, D.C. 20036

Council for Advancement and
 Support of Education (CASE)
11 Dupont Circle N.W., Suite 400
Washington, D.C. 20036

Council on Foundations, Inc.
1828 L Street N.W.
Washington, D.C. 20036

Film Fund
135 East 15 Street
New York, N.Y. 10003

Foundation for the Community of
 Artists
280 Broadway, Suite 412
New York, N.Y. 10007

Graphic Artists Guild
30 East 20 Street
New York, N.Y. 10003

Independent Sector
1828 L Street N.W.
Washington, D.C. 20036

International Society of
 Performing Arts Administrators
P.O. Box 7818
University of Texas
Austin, Tex. 78712

League of Historic American
Theaters
1600 H Street N.W.
Washington, D.C. 20006

League of Residential Theaters
Center Stage
700 North Calvert St.
Baltimore, Md. 21201

National Association for Hospital
Development
112B East Broad Street
Falls Church, Va. 22046

National Association for Regional
Ballet
1123 Broadway
New York, N.Y. 10010

National Association of Artists'
Organizations
930 F Street N.W.
Washington, D.C. 20004

National Association of Church
Business Administrators
7001 Grapevine Highway,
Suite 324
Fort Worth, Tex. 76118

National Association of Physical
Therapists
P.O. Box 367
West Covina, Calif. 91763

National Association of Social
Workers
7981 Eastern Avenue
Silver Spring, Md. 20910

National Association of
Synagogue Administrators
Adas Israel Congregation
2850 Quebec Street N.W.
Washington, D.C. 20008

National Association of Temple
Administrators
838 Fifth Avenue
New York, N.Y. 10021

National Commission on
Certification of Physicians
Assistants, Inc.
3384 Peachtree Road N.W., #560
Atlanta, Ga. 30326

National Congress for Community
Economic Development
2025 I Street N.W., Suite 901
Washington, D.C. 20006

National Education Association
1201 16 Street N.W.
Washington, D.C. 20036

National Health Lawyers
Association
522 21 Street N.W., #120
Washington, D.C. 20006

National League for Nursing
10 Columbus Circle
New York, N.Y. 10019

National Legal Center for the
Public Interest
1101 17 Street N.W.
Washington, D.C. 20036

National Network of Grantmakers
2000 P Street N.W., Suite 400
Washington, D.C. 20036

National Science Foundation
1800 G Street N.W.
Washington, D.C. 20550

National Society of Fund Raising
Executives
1511 K Street N.W.
Investment Building, Suite 1000
Washington, D.C. 20036

National Trust for Historic
Preservation
1785 Massachusetts Avenue N.W.
Washington, D.C. 20036

Public Relations Society
of America
845 Third Avenue
New York, N.Y. 10022

Society for Nonprofit
Organizations
6314 Odana Road, Suite 1
Madison, Wis. 53711

Society for Research
Administrators
1505 4 Street, Suite 203
Santa Monica, Calif. 90401

Society of American Archivists
600 South Federal, Suite 504
Chicago, Ill. 60605

Special Libraries Association
235 Park Avenue South
New York, N.Y. 10003

University and College Labor
Education Association
Department of Labor Studies
901 Liberal Arts, Pennsylvania
State University
University Park, Pa. 16802

References

PERIODICALS

AARTimes (monthly)
American Association for
 Respiration Therapy
1720 Regal Row
Dallas, Tex. 75235

AHA! Hispanic Arts News
 (monthly)
Association for Hispanic Arts
200 East 87 Street
New York, N.Y. 10028

AMERICAN JOURNAL OF
 NURSING (monthly)
American Nurses Association
2420 Pershing Road
Kansas City, Mo. 64108

AMERICAN JOURNAL OF
 OCCUPATIONAL THERAPY
 (monthly)
American Occupational Therapy
 Association
1383 Piccard Drive, Suite 301
Rockville, Md. 20850

AMERICAN JOURNAL OF
 PUBLIC HEALTH (monthly)
American Public Health
 Association
1015 15 Street N.W.
Washington, D.C. 20005

AMERICAN LIBRARIES
 (12 issues/year)
American Library Association
50 East Huron Street
Chicago, Ill. 60611

THE AMERICAN NURSE
 (monthly)
American Nurses Association
2420 Pershing Road
Kansas City, Mo. 64108

AMERICAN THEATRE
 (11 issue/year)
Theatre Communications Group,
 Inc.
355 Lexington Avenue
New York, N.Y. 10017

References   195

ART AND ARTISTS
Foundation for the Community of Artists
280 Broadway, Suite 412
New York, N.Y. 10007

ARTnews   (12 issues/year)
5 West 37 Street
New York, N.Y. 10018

ARTSEARCH   (23 issues/year (job listings))
Theatre Communications Group, Inc.
355 Lexington Avenue
New York, N.Y. 10017

ARTS INTERNATIONAL
(4 newsletters/year)
Arts International—
Bacon House Mews
606 18th Street N.W.
Washington, D.C. 20006

ARTS Review   (4 issues/year)
National Education Association
1100 Pennsylvania Avenue N.W.
Washington, D.C. 20506

CAREER LETTER   (10/year (in newsletter))
National Association for Hospital Development
112B East Broad Street
Falls Church, Va. 22046

CAREER OPPORTUNITIES NEWS
(6 issues/year)
Garrett Park Press
Garrett Park, Md. 20896

CHRONICLE OF HIGHER EDUCATION   (weekly)
1255 23 Street N.W.
Washington, D.C. 20037

CHRONICLE OF NONPROFIT ENTERPRISE   (6 issues/year)
138 Wyatt Way N.E.
Bainbridge Island, Wash. 98110

COMMUNITY JOBS
(12 issues/year)
1319 19th Street N.W.
Washington, D.C. 20036

CONSERVE NEIGHBORHOODS
(10 issues/year)
National Trust for Historic Preservation
1785 Massachusetts Avenue N.W.
Washington, D.C. 20036

CORPORATE ALTERNATIVES TODAY   (6 issues/year (no charge))
P.O. Box 1613
Springfield, Ill. 62705

COUNCIL ON FOUNDATIONS NEWSLETTER   (biweekly)
1828 L Street N.W.
Washington, D.C. 20036

CRIMINAL JUSTICE REPORTER
(monthly)
National Legal Center for the Public Interest
1101 17th Street N.W.
Washington, D.C. 20036

CURRENTS   (10 issues/year)
Council for the Advancement and Support of Secondary Education
11 Dupont Circle N.W., Suite 400
Washington, D.C. 20036

DONOR BRIEFING
(26 issues/year)
Chicago Tribune Company
Box 183, 1340 West Irving Park Road
Chicago, Ill. 60613

FILM FUND NEWSLETTER
(quarterly)
135 East 15 Street
New York, N.Y. 10003

FOUNDATION NEWS
(bimonthly)
Council on Foundations, Inc.
1828 L Street N.W.
Washington, D.C. 20036

FUNDRAISING MANAGEMENT
(monthly)
Hoke Communications, Inc.
224 Seventh Street
Garden City, N.Y. 11530

FUNDRAISING REVIEW
(6 issues/year)
AAFRC Trust for Philanthropy
25 West 43 Street
New York, N.Y. 10036

GRANTS MAGAZINE (quarterly)
Plenum Publishing Company
233 Spring Street
New York, N.Y. 10013

GRASSROOTS FUNDRAISING
   JOURNAL (6 issues/year)
P.O. Box 14754
San Francisco, Calif. 94114

GUIDEPOST
(18 newsletters/year)
American Association for
   Counseling and Development
5999 Stevenson Avenue
Alexandria, Va. 22304

HEALTH AND SOCIAL WORK
(quarterly)
National Association of Social
   Workers
7981 Eastern Avenue
Silver Spring, Md. 20910

KRC LETTER (about fund raising)
(10 issues/year)
Box 53
Hastings-on-Hudson, N.Y. 10706

LIBRARY JOURNAL (20 issues/year)
R.R. Bowker Company,
P.O. Box 1427
Riverton, N.J. 08077

LIBRARY SOFTWARE REVIEW
(6 issues/year)
Meckler Publishing Co.
11 Ferry Lane West
Westport, Conn. 06880

MONITOR (monthly)
Center for Community Change
1000 Wisconsin Avenue N.W.
Washington, D.C. 20007

NATIONAL SCIENCE
   FOUNDATION BULLETIN
(monthly; job listings)
1800 G Street N.W.
Washington, D.C. 20550

NATION'S HEALTH (monthly newspaper)
American Public Health
   Association
1015 15 Street N.W.
Washington, D.C. 20005

NEA TODAY
(9 issues/year)
National Education
   Association
1201 16 Street N.W.
Washington, D.C. 20036

NURSING AND HEALTH CARE
(10 issues/year)
National League for Nursing
10 Columbus Circle
New York, N.Y. 10019

PERFORMING ARTS FORUM
(6 newsletters/year)
International Society of Performing
   Arts Administrators
P.O. Box 7818,
University of Texas
Austin, Tex. 78712

PERSONNEL ADMINISTRATOR
(monthly)
American Society of Personnel
   Administrators
606 North Washington Street
Alexandria, Va. 22314

PERSONNEL AND GUIDANCE
   JOURNAL (10 issues/year)
American Association for
   Counseling and Development
5999 Stevenson Avenue
Alexandria, Va. 22304

PERSONNELITE (weekly newsletter)
College and University Personnel
   Association
11 Dupont Circle N.W., #120
Washington, D.C. 20036

PHILANTHROPY MONTHLY
(newsletter; job listings)
Non-Profit Report, Inc.
P.O. Box 989
New Milford, Conn. 06776

PHYSICAL THERAPY JOURNAL (monthly)
American Physical Therapy Association
1111 North Fairfax Street
Alexandria, Va. 22314

PROGRESS REPORT (monthly newsletter)
American Physical Therapy Association
1111 North Fairfax Street
Alexandria, Va. 22314

PUBLIC RELATIONS JOURNAL (monthly)
Public Relations Society of America
845 Third Avenue
New York, N.Y. 10022

RESOURCES (monthly newsletter)
National Congress for Community Economic Development
2025 I Street N.W., Suite 901
Washington, D.C. 20006

RESPIRATORY CARE (monthly)
American Association for Respiration Therapy
1720 Regal Row
Dallas, Tex. 75234

SOCIAL WORK (bimonthly)
National Association of Social Workers
7981 Eastern Avenue
Silver Spring, Md. 20910

SOCIETY OF AMERICAN ARCHIVISTS NEWSLETTER (monthly; job listings)
600 South Federal, Suite 504
Chicago, Ill. 60605

SPECIAL EVENTS (6 issues/year)
Miramar Publishing Company
2048 Cotner Avenue
Los Angeles, Calif. 90025

SPECIAL LIBRARIES (quarterly)
Special Libraries Association
235 Park Avenue South
New York, N.Y. 10003

THE TAFT NONPROFIT EXECUTIVE (monthly)
The Taft Group
5125 MacArthur Boulevard N.W.
Washington, D.C. 20016

WISE GIVING GUIDE (bimonthly)
National Charities Information Bureau, Inc.
19 Union Square West
New York, N.Y. 10003

WOMEN AND HEALTH (quarterly)
Haworth Press
28 East 22 Street
New York, N.Y. 10010

BOOKS

AMERICAN LIBRARY DIRECTORY. 38th edition. Editor: Jacques Cattell Press. New York: R.R. Bowker, 1985.

CAREERS IN HEALTH SERVICES. Seide, Diane. New York: E.P. Dutton, 1982.

CAREERS IN THE OUTDOORS. Boesch, Mark. New York: E.P. Dutton, 1975.

COMMUNITY RESOURCE DIRECTORY. A guide to U.S. voluntary organizations. 2d edition. Detroit: Gale Research Co., 1984.

DIRECTORY OF SPECIAL LIBRARIES AND INFORMATION CENTERS. 9th edition. Editor: Brigitte Darnay. Detroit: Gale Research Co., 1985.

FAST TRACK TO THE TOP JOBS IN NEW MEDICAL CAREERS. Eron, Carol. New York: Putnam Publishing Group, 1984.

GUIDE TO CAREERS IN WORLD AFFAIRS. Editors of Foreign Policy Association. New York: Foreign Policy Association, 1982.

HANDBOOK OF HEALTH CAREERS: A GUIDE TO EMPLOYMENT OPPORTUNITIES. Nassif, Janet Zhun. New York: Human Sciences Press, 1980.

HOW TO GET A FEDERAL JOB...OR SURVIVE A R.I.F. Waelde, D.E. Washington, D.C.: Fedhelp Publications, 1982.

HOW TO TEACH SCHOOL AND MAKE A LIVING AT THE SAME TIME. Crowe, Patrick H. Mission, Kans.: Sheed, Andrews & McMeed, 1978.

INTERNATIONAL DIRECTORY OF THEATRE, DANCE AND FOLKLORE FESTIVALS. Merin, Jennifer, and Burdick, Elizabeth. Westport, Conn.: Greenwood Press, 1979.

MUSICAL AMERICA. New York: ABC Leisure Magazine, Inc.

NATIONAL DIRECTORY FOR THE PERFORMING ARTS AND CIVIC CENTERS. New York: John Wiley & Sons, 1978.

NEW CAREER OPPORTUNITIES IN HEALTH AND HUMAN SERVICES. De Ridder, Margaret Djerf. New York: ARCO Publishing Co., 1984.

THE OFFICIAL MUSEUM DIRECTORY. American Association of Museums. Wilmette, Ill.: National Register Publishing Co., 1984.

ONE HUNDRED AND ONE CHALLENGING GOVERNMENT JOBS FOR COLLEGE GRADUATES. Shanahan, William F. New York: ARCO Publishing Co., 1986.

OPPORTUNITIES IN COUNSELING AND DEVELOPMENT. Baxter, Neale. Lincolnwood, Ill.: VGM Career Horizons, 1986.

OPPORTUNITIES IN COUNSELING AND GUIDANCE. Oana, Katherine. Lincolnwood, Ill.: VGM Career Horizons, 1979.

OPPORTUNITIES IN ENVIRONMENTAL CAREERS. Fanning, Odom. Lincolnwood, Ill.: VGM Career Horizons, 1986.

OPPORTUNITIES IN FEDERAL GOVERNMENT CAREERS. Baxter, Neale. Lincolnwood, Ill.: VGM Career Horizons, 1985.

OPPORTUNITIES IN FOOD SERVICE. Caprione, Carol Ann. Lincolnwood, Ill.: VGM Career Horizons, 1984.

OPPORTUNITIES IN HEALTH AND MEDICAL CAREERS. Snook, I. Donald, Jr., and D'Orazio, Lee D. Lincolnwood, Ill.: VGM Career Horizons, 1985.

OPPORTUNITIES IN HOSPITAL ADMINISTRATION. Snook, I. Donald, Jr. Lincolnwood, Ill.: VGM Career Horizons, 1982.

OPPORTUNITIES IN LAW CAREERS. Munneke, Gary A. Lincolnwood, Ill.: VGM Career Horizons, 1982.

OPPORTUNITIES IN LIBRARY AND INFORMATION SCIENCE. Heim, Kathleen, and Sullivan, Peggy. Lincolnwood, Ill.: VGM Career Horizons, 1985.

OPPORTUNITIES IN MUSIC CAREERS. Gerardi, Robert. Lincolnwood, Ill.: VGM Career Horizons, 1985.

OPPORTUNITIES IN NUTRITION CAREERS. Caldwell, Carol. Lincolnwood, Ill.: VGM Career Horizons, 1986.

OPPORTUNITIES IN PARAMEDICAL CAREERS. Kacen, Alex. Lincolnwood, Ill.: VGM Career Horizons, 1985.

OPPORTUNITIES IN SPORTS MEDICINE. Heitzmann, William Ray. Lincolnwood, Ill.: VGM Career Horizons, 1985.

OPPORTUNITIES IN STATE AND LOCAL GOVERNMENT CAREERS. Baxter, Neale. Lincolnwood, Ill.: VGM Career Horizons, 1985.

ORPHEUS IN THE NEW WORLD. Hart, Philip. New York: W.W. Norton & Co., 1973.

PERFORMING ARTS DIRECTORY. DANCE Magazine annual. New York: DANCE Magazine.

THE PHYSICIAN'S ASSOCIATE—A NEW CAREER IN HEALTH CARE. Cavallaro, Ann. New York: Elsevier/Nelson Books, 1978.

SURVEY OF ARTS ADMINISTRATION TRAINING IN THE U.S. AND CANADA. New York: American Council for the Arts, 1977.

TEACHER. Rudman, Jack. Syosset, N.Y.: National Learning Corp., 1977.

THEATRE PROFILES: THE ILLUSTRATED REFERENCE GUIDE TO AMERICAN'S NONPROFIT THEATRES. New York: Theatre Communications Group, 1982.

THE UNCLE SAM CONNECTION. Hawkins, James. Chicago: Follett Publishing Co., 1978.

WHO'S WHO IN SPECIAL LIBRARIES 1985–86. Washington, D.C.: Special Libraries Assoc.

YOUR CAREER IN THE FOREIGN SERVICE. Berman, Susanna. New York: ARCO Publishing Co., 1983.

YOUR FUTURE IN LIBRARY CAREERS. Myers, Alpha, and Temkin, Sara. New York: ARCO Publishing Co., 1976.

Index

Administration, 148–158
Administrative assistants, 149–151
Administrative dietitian, 96
American Association of Fund-Raising Counsel, 9-10
American Bar Association, 14
American Dietetic Association Journal, 97
American Friends Service Committee, 16
American Institute of Certified Public Accountants, 14
American Medical Association, 14
Arts, 10
Arts organization consultant, 110–112
Associations, listing of, 190–193
Attorneys. *See* Lawyers

Benefits coordinator, 100–102
Business Committee for the Arts, 8

Catalogers, 69
CATALYST, 174
Certified Fund-Raising Executive (CFRE), 59
Chief executive officer (CEO), 27–46
Children's Defense Fund, 45
Children's librarian, 69
Chronicle of Higher Education, 175
Civic groups, 10
Clinical dietitian, 96
Committee for Dignity and Fairness for the Homeless, 44
Community coordinator, 71–73
Community Jobs, The Public Interest Clearinghouse Employment Report, 63
Computer Museum in Boston, 7
Contributions, 48
Counseling, 77–82

Dayton–Hudson Company, 8
Development office, 47–60
   functions of, 48–49
   qualifications and training for, 49–53
Dietitians, 96–98
Direct mail, 57, 58–59

Education, 10–11
   elementary, 73–84
   higher, 102–106
   public relations in, 137–139
   secondary, 73–84
   special, 82–83
Educational association, 107–110
Employment agencies, 185
Ethical Culture Society, 13
Executive director, 27–46
   becoming an, 41–46
   benefits of, 39–41
   characteristics of, 29–32
   evaluating position of, 32–41
   management style of, 35–37
   salary of, 39–41
   and size of organization, 37–39

Family counseling, 81
Federal Bureau of Investigation, 167
Federal Career Opportunities, 165
Federal Jobs Digest, 165
Federal positions, 159–169
501(c)3 groups, 3
Ford Foundation, 13
Foreign Service, 168–169
Foundation Center, 21, 66, 67, 68, 70
Foundation for the Extension and Development of American Professional Theater (FEDAPT), 110–112
Foundation for Long-Term Care, 7
Foundations, 13
Fund raising, 49, 53–60
Fund Raising Management, 175

General Accounting Office, 167–168
General Printing Office, 168
Geriatric counseling, 81
Girl Scouts of the United States of America, 6
Government positions, 159–171
Graphic Artists Guild, 127

Hartford Architecture Conservancy, 7
Health services, 10, 11, 85–92
Homeless population, 12–13
Hospice, 90
Hospitals, 10, 11
   social work at, 63–66

Information broker, 71
Informational interviewing, 177–183
Inhalation therapist, 92–93
Interviewing, 186–189

Job ads, 184–185
Junto Organization, 9

Labor unions, 13–14
Lawyers, 61–63
Librarian, 66–71
Lobbying, 3, 109
Local government positions, 170–171

Management styles, 23
   of executive director, 35–37
March of Dimes, 11, 13
Marketing, 57–58
Marriage counseling, 81
Membership, 113–124
Modern Language Association, 14
Museum of Broadcasting, 7
Museum News, 175

National Association for the Advancement of Colored People (NAACP), 11–12

National Charities Information
    Bureau (NCIB), 4, 186
*National and Federal Legal
    Employment Report*, 63, 164
National Society of Fund-Raising
    Executives, 59
Networking, 177–184
New Mexico Museum of Natural
    History, 7
New Ventures, 7
Nonprofit employees, 15–26
    traits of, 15–17
Nonprofit workplace, 17–24
Nonprofits
    difference from corporations,
        1–4
    history of, 8–9
North Wind Underseas Institute, 7
Not for profit, definition of, 1
*Now Hiring: Government Jobs for
    Lawyers*, 164
Nurses. *See* Health service

Occupational Outlook Handbook, 174
Occupational therapist, 95–96
Oram Group, 16

Pastoral counseling, 81
Peoples Firehouse, 44, 125
Periodicals, listing of, 194–199
Philanthropy, 8, 9
Physical therapist, 98–100
Physician's assistant, 93–95
Planned giving, 57
Plants and Gardens, 132, 133
Preservation Maryland, 39
Princess Grace Foundation, 8, 13
Procurement specialists, 167
Professional organizations, 176–177
Program department, 61–112
Public groups, 10
Public relations, 136–147
Publications, 125–135

Reference librarian, 69
Rehabilitation counselors, 80
Religious organizations, 10
Research dietitian, 97
Respiration therapist, 92–93

Salaries, 53
    of executive director, 39–41
    of government positions, 161,
        164
Secretaries, 149–151
Serials librarian, 69
Slide librarian, 69
Smithsonian Institution, 8
Social Security system, 166
Social welfare, 10
Social work
    at hospital, 63–66
Special education, 82–83
Sports medicine, 99
Starlight Foundation, 7
State government positions,
    170–171
Systems librarian, 69

Teachers. *See* Education
Trade associations, 14
Treehouse Wildlife Center, 6–7

Unions. *See* Labor unions
United Federation of Teachers
    (UFT), 139, 140, 141
United Negro College Fund, 13
U.S. Lighthouse Society, 7
U.S. Post Office, 166

Values inventory, 25–26
Veterans Administration, 167
Volunteering, 185–186

Wellness Community, 71, 72, 73